Hroswitha of Gandersheim

Her Life, Times, and Works, and a Comprehensive Bibliography

PORTRAIT OF HROSWITHA OF GANDERSHEIM.
Engraved plate from Johann Georg Leuckfeld, *Antiquitates Gandersheimenses*,
Wolfenbüttel, 1709

Hroswitha of Gandersheim

~ HER LIFE, TIMES, AND WORKS, AND
A COMPREHENSIVE BIBLIOGRAPHY

Edited by Anne Lyon Haight

The Hroswitha Club · *New York, 1965*

Copyright © 1965 by the Hroswitha Club, New York
Library of Congress Catalog Card Number 65–29081
Distributed by Stechert-Hafner, Inc.
31 East Tenth Street, New York, N. Y.
Printed and bound by Clarke & Way, Inc., New York

In memory of
RACHEL MCMASTERS MILLER HUNT,
a founder and past president of the Hroswitha Club,
who was herself
a distinguished collector and bibliophile.

Table of Contents

Foreword   *ix*

Hroswitha of Gandersheim:
    Her Life, Her Times, Her Works   3
      Anne Lyon Haight

Performances of Hroswitha's Plays   35
      Marjorie Dana Barlow

The Manuscripts   42
      Meta Harrsen

Lost Manuscripts   54
      Meta Harrsen

Printed Editions, Including Translations   57
      Marjorie Dana Barlow

References to Hroswitha and Her Writing   78
      Marjorie Dana Barlow

Index   119

Foreword

In 1944 Mrs. Robert Herndon Fife of New York conceived the idea of founding a women's book collectors club to provide an opportunity for congenial bibliophiles to exchange ideas and knowledge about books and collecting. She asked the following collectors and scholars to meet with her: Mrs. Roy Arthur Hunt, Mrs. Allan Marquand, Miss Belle da Costa Greene, Miss Henrietta C. Bartlett, Miss Ruth Grannis, and Mrs. Sherman Post Haight. As a result they established the Hroswitha Club, named after the tenth century canoness of the Abbey of Gandersheim, Saxony, the most remarkable poet, dramatist, and historian of her time in Germany.

In 1947 Dr. Robert Herndon Fife, Professor of Germanic Studies at Columbia University, was commissioned by the club to write the life of Hroswitha. This delightful essay stimulated so much interest in the canoness that it was decided to collect books by and about her.

In 1949 Mrs. Hunt laid the cornerstone of the club library with the gift of the first edition (second issue) of the *Opera* of Hroswitha, edited by Conrad Celtes, Nuremberg, 1501 (No. 15). Subsequently many other books of importance were donated by members to the library.

In order to build this library it was necessary to have an up-to-date bibliography of the books desired. In 1947 Edwin Zeydel had published "A chronological Hrotsvitha bibliography through 1700, with annotations" in *The Journal of English and Germanic Philology*, Vol. 46, July, 1947 (No. 284), which, in view of recent findings, was far from complete. Fortunately for the Hroswitha Club, a member, Marjorie

Dana Barlow, assumed the arduous task of augmenting the list. Mrs. Barlow, an experienced bibliographer and collector, spent years in collecting the material for the check list from the key libraries of the world.

Mrs. Barlow also made a tentative list of the known performances of Hroswitha's plays. There have been many conjectures as to whether they were acted during her lifetime and the answer will probably never be known. However, it is interesting to note that the dramatic effectiveness of her plays has been demonstrated in the many performances that have been given in various countries through the years.

It was most important to establish the authenticity of Hroswitha's manuscripts, since, over one hundred years ago, an Austrian historian, Joseph Aschbach, conceived the idea that Hroswitha had never existed and that her works were the figment of the imagination of Conrad Celtes, humanist poet of Germany. Aschbach contended that Hroswitha's worldly knowledge was too great and her latinity too perfect for a cloistered canoness of the period. This started a long-enduring controversy which could have been solved had anyone made a paleographical examination of the known manuscripts. It remained for the Hroswitha Club to do so.

Happily, a member, Miss Meta Harrsen, Keeper Emeritus of Manuscripts at the Pierpont Morgan Library, in spite of her important professional commitments, was kind enough to make the first paleographical examination of the eight manuscripts, and to write a descriptive critique of each one which conclusively established their authenticity once and for all. Miss Harrsen also compiled a list of the lost manuscripts.

The bibliography of manuscripts and printed books wasr echecked and set up for publication by the late Miss Jane Quinby, librarian of the Hroswitha Club. She was a well-known professional bibliographer of standing, and worked faithfully, in spite of illness, for several years on this labor of love.

Miss Quinby also edited the notes and summaries prepared by János Scholz in connection with his translation of Hroswitha's *Dulcitius* as it appeared in the *Sándor Codex*. Mr. Scholz, Hungarian scholar, musician, and collector is owed a great debt of gratitude for making this first English translation from the medieval Hungarian of the sixteenth century.

Hroswitha of Gandersheim: Her Life, Her Times, Her Works has been written as a background to the bibliography, in an effort to describe the environment that influenced her writings. She was surrounded by the splendor of the Ottonian era, and benefited from the cultural and educational excellence which prevailed in monasteries such as Gandersheim. The prefaces and dedications have been included as they reveal more of the character and personality of Hroswitha than can be derived from any other source. Included also is a summary of her works with notes.

ACKNOWLEDGMENTS

In addition to the club members already mentioned, several others contributed greatly in gathering information for this book. Mrs. Roy Hunt arranged for research to be done in Germany on the Hroswitha manuscripts, and had them photographed. Mrs. Robert Woods Bliss commissioned Mrs. Natalie Scheffer to make a summary of Dr. V. A. Bilbasov's scholarly Russian refutation of Aschbach's allegation of the nonauthenticity of Hroswitha and her works, (St. Petersburg, 1873). Of special importance have been Miss Julia Wightman's gifts of books, including *Antiquitates Gandersheimenses* by Johann Georg Leuckfeld, 1709 (No. 21), which contains the first complete printing of the *Primordia*, as well as many of the plates reproduced in this book.

Dr. Karl Vogel has rendered invaluable assistance in translating many books and pamphlets from the German for me. I am also sincerely grateful to Canon Edward N. West, of the Cathedral of St. John the Divine, for reading and correcting my essay, *Hroswitha of Gandersheim: Her Life, Her Times, Her Works*.

Miss Quinby was very appreciative of the assistance given by her advisory committee in the setting up of the over-all presentation of the bibliography of the printed books for the maximum usefulness to research students. The advisory council consisted of:

Lewis H. Stark, *New York Public Library, Chief, Reserve Division*
Allen T. Hazen, *Bibliographer and Professor of English at Columbia University*

William A. Jackson, *Harvard College, Professor of Bibliography and Librarian of the Houghton Library*
Frederick R. Goff, *Library of Congress, Chief, Rare Book Division*
Margaret B. Stillwell, *member of Hroswitha Club, Professor of Bibliography at Brown University, and Librarian Emeritus of the Ann Mary Brown Memorial Library.*

The bibliographies of *Printed Editions* of works by Hroswitha and of *References to Hroswitha and Her Writing* could not have been compiled without the generous assistance of so many libraries both here and abroad. In reply to Mrs. Barlow's requests they sent long lists of their holdings of Hroswitha material and often supplied photographs and additional information about specific items. Libraries which were especially helpful include:

UNITED STATES:
   California: Henry E. Huntington Library, San Marino
   Connecticut: Yale University Library, New Haven
   District of Columbia: Catholic University of America Library, Washington; Library of Congress, Washington
   Maryland: Johns Hopkins University Library, Baltimore; Peabody Institute, Baltimore; Walters Art Gallery, Baltimore
   Massachusetts: Boston Medical Library, Boston; Boston Public Library, Boston; Harvard University Library, Cambridge; Williams College, Chapin Library, Williamstown
   Michigan: Michigan State University Library, East Lansing
   Missouri: St. Louis University Library, St. Louis
   New Hampshire: Dartmouth College, Baker Library, Hanover
   New Jersey: Princeton University Library, Princeton
   New York: Columbia University Library, New York; Cornell University Library, Ithaca; Fordham University Library, New York; Metropolitan Museum of Art Library, New York; New York Public Library, New York; New York State University Library, Albany; New York University, University Heights Library, New York; Pierpont Morgan Library, New York

Ohio: Cleveland Public Library, Cleveland
Pennsylvania: Bryn Mawr College Library, Bryn Mawr;
    University of Pennsylvania Library, Philadelphia
Rhode Island: Ann Mary Brown Memorial Library, Providence

Europe:
    Amsterdam: Universiteits-Bibliotheek, Holland
    Berlin: Deutsche Staatsbibliothek, Germany
    Bologna: Biblioteca Universitaria, Italy
    Brussels: Bibliothèque Royale de Belgique, Belgium
    Budapest: Egyetemi Könyvtár (University Library), Hungary
    Cologne: Universitäts-und Stadtbibliothek, Köln-Lindenthal,
        Germany
    Copenhagen: Det Kongelige Bibliothek, Denmark
    Dublin: Catholic Library Information Bureau, Ireland
    Florence: Biblioteca Nazionale Centrale, Italy
    Ghent: Rijksuniversiteit Centrale Bibliotheek, Belgium
    Gothenburg: Gothenburg Stadsbibliotek, Sweden
    Gottingen: Niedersächsische Staats-und Universitätsbibliothek,
        Germany
    Hamburg: Staats-und Universitäts Bibliothek, Germany
    Heidelberg: Universitätsbibliothek, Germany
    Jena: Universitätsbibliothek, Germany
    Leipzig: Karl-Marx-Universitätsbibliothek, Germany
    Leningrad: Leningrad State University, M. Gorky Scientific
        Library, U.S.S.R.; M. E. Saltykov-Schedrin State Public
        Library, U.S.S.R.
    London: British Museum, England; Women's Service Library
        of the Fawcett Society, England
    Louvain: Bibliothèque de l'Université, Belgium
    Milan: Biblioteca Ambrosiana, Italy; Museo Teatrale alla
        Scala, Italy
    Moscow: State Library of the Order of Lenin, U.S.S.R.
    Munich: Bayerische Staatsbibliothek, Germany
    Oslo: Universitetsbiblioteket, Norway
    Oxford: Oxford University, Bodleian Library, England

xiii

Paris: Bibliothèque Nationale, France; Université de Paris, Bibliothèque Sainte Geneviève, France

Prague: Státni knihovna CSR-Universitní knihovan (State Library of the Czechoslovak Republic, University Library), Czechoslovakia

Rome: Biblioteca Nazionale Centrale, Vittorio Emanuele II, Italy; Biblioteca Vaticana, Vatican City, Italy

St. Florian b. Linz: Stiftsbibliothek, Chorherrenstift, Austria

St. Gallen: Stiftsbibliothek, Switzerland

Tübingen: Universitätsbibliothek Tübingen, Depot der ehem Preussische Staatsbibliothek, Germany

Uppsala: Universitetsbiblioteket, Sweden

Venice: Biblioteca Nazionale di S. Marco, Italy

Vienna: Österreichische National-Bibliothek, Austria

Wolfenbüttel: Herzog August Bibliothek, Germany

Würzburg: Universitätsbibliothek, Germany

And finally, it is to be noted that this volume might never have been published were it not for the continued interest and generosity of Roy Arthur Hunt, whose gift to the Hroswitha Club in memory of his wife, the late Rachel McMasters Miller Hunt, made this publication possible. To Roy Hunt the Hroswitha Club acknowledges its thanks and gratitude.

ANNE LYON HAIGHT, *President*
The Hroswitha Club, New York

Hroswitha of Gandersheim

Hroswitha of Gandersheim

Her Life, Her Times, Her Works

ANNE LYON HAIGHT

The most remarkable woman of her time was Hroswitha, the tenth-century canoness of the Benedictine monastery of Gandersheim, Saxony. She was the earliest poet known in Germany and the first dramatist after the fall of the ancient stage of classical times.

In 1494 Conrad Celtes, the Renaissance humanist and first poet laureate of Germany, found an early and incomplete manuscript (*Munich Codex*; see pp. 42–43) of the work of this "German Sappho," as he called her, in the monastery of Saint Emmeram at Regensburg. He published it in 1501, but unfortunately changed the order of her works and made "corrections." It had been lying forgotten for almost six hundred years and her name had slipped into obscurity.

Her writings, as far as they are known, include eight sacred legends in verse, six dramas in rhymed prose, two historical poems, three prose prefaces, several dedications, and finally a poem which compresses *The Revelation [Vision] of St. John* into thirty-five lines. His Eminence Cardinal Gasquet said of her: "Hroswitha's works have a claim to an eminent place in medieval literature, and do honour to her sex, to the age in which she lived, and to the vocation which she followed."

All we know of this gifted poet is what she tells us in her writings, and what the historians have pieced together by aligning their contents with the scant annals of her time. It has been deduced that she was born about 935, for she says in a preface that her Abbess, the Princess Gerberga, whose known date of birth was 940, was younger than she. The date of her death is also uncertain, but has been placed about 1001–1002.

The tenth century has been called the Dark Ages, but due to the Carolingian renaissance, Germany had become a country of enlightenment and learning. Although it was only at the end of the eighth century that the tribes accepted Christianity—Saxony being the last to do so—thus submitting to Charlemagne's grim threat of acceptance or death, the chieftains, within a few decades, were forgetting paganism and were building churches and endowing monasteries under native bishops.

At the end of the ninth century twenty cloisters were recorded in Saxony, eleven of them nunneries—containing both Benedictine straight nuns and canonesses. One of the first was Gandersheim, the Abbey of Hroswitha, who was to record its history later in her historical poem *Primordia Coenobii Gandeshemensis*. It was established first at Brunshausen on the River Gande; later Bishop Altfrid laid the cornerstone of Gandersheim at a more advantageous site about twenty miles from the present city of Hildesheim. The monastery was consecrated on All Saints' Day in 881. Thankmar wrote about the canonesses being moved at that time from Brunshausen to Gandersheim, although some of the nuns were presumed to have remained behind for a time.

The monastery was founded by Duke Liudolf at the request of his Frankish wife Oda and her mother Aeda. Hroswitha

LIUDOLF, founder of the monastery of Gandersheim. Engraved plate from Johann Georg
Leuckfeld, *Antiquitates Gandersheimenses*, Wolfenbüttel, 1709.

LIUDOLF AND ODA, founders of the monastery of Gandersheim. Engraved plate from Johann Georg Leuckfeld, *Antiquitates Gandersheimenses*, Wolfenbüttel, 1709.

says in her *Primordia* that Liudolf was, from his earliest years, in the service of the great Louis I, King of the Franks, and was elevated by him to distinguished honors. Aeda, who was deeply religious, had been visited by a vision of Saint John the Baptist who informed her that her famous progeny would someday establish a cloister for saintly maidens. Consequently, Liudolf and Oda made a pilgrimage to Rome to acquire sacred relics and receive the blessing of Pope Sergius II. They petitioned the Frankish King Louis (Ludovic the German, grandson of Charlemagne) for an introduction to the Pope, fitted out a large traveling retinue, and prepared valuable presents. Much impressed with the Duke and his Lady (Hroswitha recounts), the Pope gave them the bones "of two mighty shepherds, Anastasius, the most holy bishop of his throne, and his co-apostle, the sacred Innocent." The holy relics were carried in triumph to Saxony, and Anastasius and Innocent became the patron saints of Gandersheim. The monastery became one of the richest and most distinguished of the convents founded by Liudolf, whose descendants formed the dynasty that ruled Germany in Hroswitha's time. His son Otto the Illustrious lived to see the monastery completed.

Members of the families of the great Saxon patrons often entered their religious establishments, and the first three Abbesses of Gandersheim were daughters of Liudolf and Oda. Hathmodo, the eldest, was born in 840 and was consecrated in 852 at the age of twelve. Goetting, in his *Die Anfaenge*, says that she was sent to be educated in the convent of Herford, which was from the beginning closely connected with the Kloster Corvey, where her brother Agius was a monk. Herford became the model for the many Saxon *Kanonissenstifte*, founded later. Agius also tells about Herford in his *Vita*.

Hathmodo was followed as Abbess at Gandersheim by her

7

sisters Gerberga I and by Christine, who died in 919. They in turn were followed by Hroswitha I* and Wendelgard, and it was not until Princess Gerberga II became Abbess in 959 that a member of the royal family ruled again. Gerberga II, the friend and teacher of Hroswitha, was the daughter of Henry, Duke of Bavaria, the niece of Otto I, Henry's brother, and the granddaughter of the great Saxon king, Henry the Fowler, who ruled from 919 to 936. Having won leadership by checking the raids of the wild Hungarians and driving back the heathen Slavs, Henry, the Duke of Bavaria, was given the crown and sceptre by Eberhard, Duke of the Franks, after the death of his brother Conrad, King of Germany.

Otto I, following in his father Henry's footsteps, defeated their enemies once and for all, quelled civil war, conquered northern Italy, and was crowned King of the Lombards in Pavia, the capital, where in 951 he married Adelaide, widow of the Italian King Lothar II (his first wife Edith of England had died a few years before). The following year Otto I received the Imperial Crown from Pope John XII in appreciation for restoring law and order in Italy, and became the founder of the Holy Roman Empire of the German people. Under him the arts flourished and books were penned. He was a great statesman, a patron of learning, and a benefactor of the church, although he deposed Pope John XII for treachery.

Hroswitha wrote the *Gesta Ottonis*, a history of his reign. In Celtes' 1501 publication of her works, Albrecht Dürer pictured her kneeling before the Emperor to present her book while the Abbess Gerberga II looked on. It was during this reign, when Wendelgard was Abbess, that Hroswitha entered

---

*Hroswitha I, the fourth Abbess of Gandersheim, ruled from 919 to 926. It is not known if she was related in any way to the canoness Hroswitha who is the subject of this book.

The Ottonian Dynasty, 9th and 10th Centuries

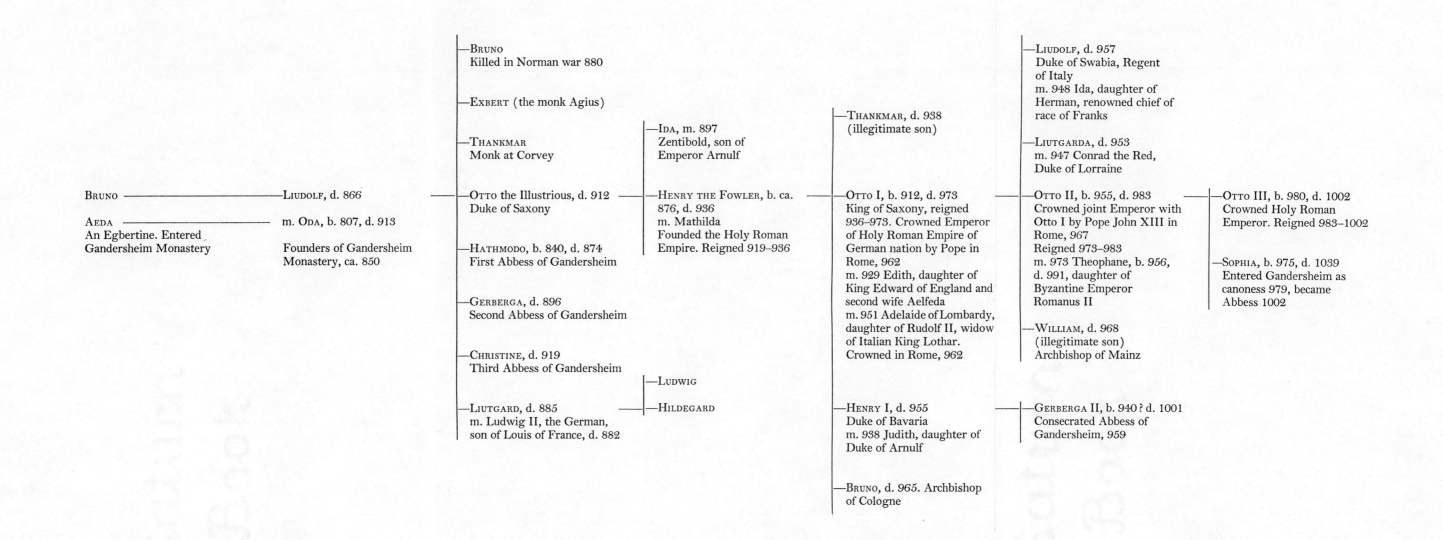

BRUNO
AEDA
An Egbertine. Entered
Gandersheim Monastery

LIUDOLF, d. 866
m. ODA, b. 807, d. 913
Founders of Gandersheim
Monastery, ca. 850

—BRUNO
Killed in Norman war 880

—EXBERT (the monk Agius)

—THANKMAR
Monk at Corvey

—OTTO the Illustrious, d. 912
Duke of Saxony

—HATHMODO, b. 840, d. 874
First Abbess of Gandersheim

—GERBERGA, d. 896
Second Abbess of Gandersheim

—CHRISTINE, d. 919
Third Abbess of Gandersheim

—LIUTGARD, d. 885
m. Ludwig II, the German,
son of Louis of France, d. 882

—IDA, m. 897
Zentibold, son of
Emperor Arnulf

—HENRY THE FOWLER, b. ca.
876, d. 936
m. Mathilda
Founded the Holy Roman
Empire. Reigned 919–936

—LUDWIG
—HILDEGARD

—THANKMAR, d. 938
(illegitimate son)

—OTTO I, b. 912, d. 973
King of Saxony, reigned
936–973. Crowned Emperor
of Holy Roman Empire of
German nation by Pope in
Rome, 962
m. 929 Edith, daughter of
King Edward of England and
second wife Aelfeda
m. 951 Adelaide of Lombardy,
daughter of Rudolf II, widow
of Italian King Lothar.
Crowned in Rome, 962

—HENRY I, d. 955
Duke of Bavaria
m. 938 Judith, daughter of
Duke of Arnulf

—BRUNO, d. 965. Archbishop
of Cologne

—LIUDOLF, d. 957
Duke of Swabia, Regent
of Italy
m. 948 Ida, daughter of
Herman, renowned chief of
race of Franks

—LIUTGARDA, d. 953
m. 947 Conrad the Red,
Duke of Lorraine

—OTTO II, b. 955, d. 983
Crowned joint Emperor with
Otto I by Pope John XIII in
Rome, 967
Reigned 973–983
m. 973 Theophane, b. 956,
d. 991, daughter of
Byzantine Emperor
Romanus II

—WILLIAM, d. 968
(illegitimate son)
Archbishop of Mainz

—GERBERGA II, b. 940? d. 1001
Consecrated Abbess of
Gandersheim, 959

—OTTO III, b. 980, d. 1002
Crowned Holy Roman
Emperor. Reigned 983–1002

—SOPHIA, b. 975, d. 1039
Entered Gandersheim as
canoness 979, became
Abbess 1002

the monastery. If the conjecture is correct that it was in 955, it was the year in which Otto II was born. Later Hroswitha and Otto II were to become great friends.

Otto II, who was also crowned Holy Roman Emperor to rule jointly with his father, married Theophano, daughter of the Byzantine Emperor Romanus II. She had great influence and introduced many refinements from the court at Constantinople, such as the wearing of silks and the taking of baths, as well as Greek art and customs. After the death of Otto II in 983, Theophano ruled for Otto III as co-regent with the boy's grandmother, Adelaide.

It is interesting to note the various foreign influences introduced into the monastery during the reign of the three Ottos through their conquests and their marriages. Archbishop Bruno of Cologne brought many scholars to Gandersheim, where they contributed to the atmosphere of learning and literary activity which surrounded Hroswitha. She tells of her association with the scholars, churchmen, and royal personages who came and went, for the court and monastery were closely allied. We know that Greek was taught to the Abbess Gerberga and her sister Hedwig, and it is possible that Hroswitha learned the language as well, for she used Greek sources for some of her stories.

Gandersheim was a free Abbey, which means that the Abbess was directly responsible to the King rather than to the church. However, in 947 Otto I freed the Abbey from royal rule and gave the Abbess supreme authority. She had her court of law, sent her men-at-arms to battle, coined her own money (some of which is still extant), and had a right to a seat in the Imperial Diet. Goetting, Algermissen, and other historians of the ninth- and tenth-century cloisters refer to Gandersheim as containing Benedictine straight nuns as well

9

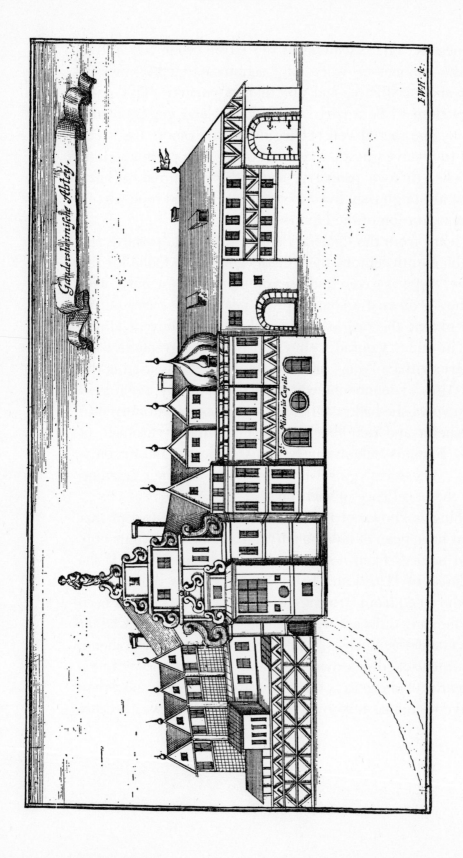

GANDERSHEIM ABBEY.
Engraved plate from Johann Georg Leuckfeld, *Antiquitates Gandersheimenses*, Wolfenbüttel, 1709.

The Ottonian Dynasty, 9th and 10th Centuri

BRUNO ——————————————————LIUDOLF, d. 866

AEDA ————————————— m. ODA, b. 807, d. 913
An Egbertine. Entered
Gandersheim Monastery   Founders of Gandersheim
                                     Monastery, ca. 850

—BRUNO
Killed in Norman war 880

—EXBERT (the monk Agius)

—THANKMAR   —IDA, m. 897   —THANKMAR, d. 938
Monk at Corvey   Zentibold, son of   (illegitimate son)
                             Emperor Arnulf

—OTTO the Illustrious, d. 912 ——— —HENRY THE FOWLER, b. ca. ——— —OTTO I, b. 912, d. 973
Duke of Saxony   876, d. 936   King of Saxony, reigned
                             m. Mathilda   936–973. Crowned Emperor
                             Founded the Holy Roman   of Holy Roman Empire of
—HATHMODO, b. 840, d. 874   Empire. Reigned 919–936   German nation by Pope in
First Abbess of Gandersheim   Rome, 962
                                                             m. 929 Edith, daughter of
                                                             King Edward of England and
—GERBERGA, d. 896   second wife Aelfeda
Second Abbess of Gandersheim   m. 951 Adelaide of Lombardy,
                                                             daughter of Rudolf II, widow
                                                             of Italian King Lothar.
—CHRISTINE, d. 919   Crowned in Rome, 962
Third Abbess of Gandersheim
                             —LUDWIG

—LIUTGARD, d. 885   ——— —HILDEGARD   —HENRY I, d. 955
m. Ludwig II, the German,   Duke of Bavaria
son of Louis of France, d. 882   m. 938 Judith, daughter of
                                                             Duke of Arnulf

                                                             —BRUNO, d. 965. Archbishop
                                                             of Cologne

—LIUDOLF, d. 957
Duke of Swabia, Regent
of Italy
m. 948 Ida, daughter of
Herman, renowned chief of
race of Franks

—LIUTGARDA, d. 953
m. 947 Conrad the Red,
Duke of Lorraine

—OTTO II, b. 955, d. 983 ———————
Crowned joint Emperor with
Otto I by Pope John XIII in
Rome, 967
Reigned 973–983
m. 973 Theophane, b. 956,
d. 991, daughter of
Byzantine Emperor
Romanus II

—WILLIAM, d. 968
(illegitimate son)
Archbishop of Mainz

—OTTO III, b. 980, d. 1002
Crowned Holy Roman
Emperor. Reigned 983–1002

—SOPHIA, b. 975, d. 1039
Entered Gandersheim as
canoness 979, became
Abbess 1002

—GERBERGA II, b. 940? d. 1001
Consecrated Abbess of
Gandersheim, 959

as canonesses. The discipline of the latter order was not as strict; the canonesses were only required to take vows of chastity and obedience, and not that of poverty. This gave them freedom to be a part of the world, and yet protected from it by the sacred veil of virginity. The canonesses were allowed to receive guests, to go and come with permission, to own books, to own property, and were permitted to have servants, although they lived a communal life and took part in the daily recitation of the Divine Office.

We learn from the *Catholic Encyclopedia* that "towards the end of the eighth century the title of canoness is found for the first time, and was given to those communities of women, who while they professed a common life, yet did not carry out to the full extent the original rule of Saint Anthony of Hippo written in 423." Conrad Celtes and other biographers have called Hroswitha a "nun" as the term was broadly used in the Middle Ages to denote one who lived in a nunnery, regardless of which vows she had taken. The priest Eberhard referred to Gandersheim and neighboring convents in his chronicle of 1215 as "Kanonissenkonvent, Kanonissenkloster and Kanonissenstift." These convents were renowned for their learning and for the excellence of their dedicated teachers.

Nothing is known of Hroswitha's background except that she must have been of noble birth: the canoness convents only accepted novices from noble families. It is not known if she was related to Hroswitha I, the fourth Abbess of Gandersheim, who ruled from 919 to 926. Hroswitha's name has been spelled in many different ways, but she called herself "Clamor Validus Gandersheimensis," the strong voice of Gandersheim, and she mentioned her own name six times in her writings. Dr. Kurt Kronenberg says that the reason her name and works may have remained unknown for so many years was because

11

before the twelfth century it was not the custom to record the names of any except highly placed persons, such as royalty and church dignitaries; although Hroswitha was a great scholar who made Gandersheim famous, she was only a canoness.

She probably entered the cloister when very young, as her skill in Latin points to many years of training under teachers well versed in Latin prosody. Her knowledge of classical and religious literature is evidence that Gandersheim had a rich collection of manuscripts, and the library must have been the center of her intellectual life in the cloister. Dr. Robert Fife said: "Judged by any standard Hroswitha's range of reading was wide and diversified and must have included Virgil's *Aeneid*, and possibly the *Georgics*, the *Eclogues*, Ovid's *Metamorphoses* and Terence's comedies, which she informs us influenced the writing of her plays. She probably read the writers of the early Christian centuries like Prudentius and Venantius Fortunatus. Above all, she seems to be indebted to the great Roman philosopher and statesman of the sixth century, Boethius, whose adherence to Christianity is much doubted by modern historians, but whom Hroswitha's contemporaries revered as a martyr to the Faith. She certainly had some introduction into Scholastic philosophy, mathematics, astronomy and especially music, of which she has shown technical knowledge. But what her young imagination seized upon most avidly was the Apocryphal stories of Christ and the Apostles and above all, the legends of the Saints, familiar reading in the churches and the cloisters of the Middle Ages." The legends, reflecting the triumphs in purity of many martyrs through their faith, filled her with religious ecstasy which is echoed in her solemn and impassioned verse. To her, chastity was the crown of the holy life.

Except for a few intercalated stanzas, Hroswitha's poetry is all in the heroic measures of the classical world, the dactylic hexameter, or in the elegiac verse, composed of two-lined strophes alternately dactylic hexameter and pentameter. She took her patterns from Virgil and the classical authors, but used the rhymed modification that was popular among early medieval writers.

There is no doubt that Hroswitha wrote the eight legends in verse first. The first five were written with a preface and a dedication to Gerberga II, and the last three carried an additional dedication. This modest poet tells in her self-revealing preface, as translated by Sister M. Gonsalva Wiegand, O.S.F.:

This little volume, adorned with but slight charm of style, but nevertheless labored upon, with no little effort, I offer for the criticism of those kindly and learned minds who take pleasure, not in exposing to ridicule a writer's faults but rather in correcting them. For I admit that I have made many errors not only in prosody but also in literary composition, and that there is much to be discovered in this collection which is deserving of severe censure. But by admitting my shortcomings I may expect a ready pardon, and a kindly correction of my errors.

Moreover, if the objection is made that, according to the judgment of some, portions of this work have been borrowed from Apocryphal sources, to this I would answer that I have erred through ignorance and not through reprehensible presumption. For when I started to weave the thread of this collection, I was not aware of the fact that the authenticity of the material upon which I planned to work was questionable. When I discovered the real state of affairs, I declined to discard my subject matter, on the plea that what appears to be false, may eventually be proved to be true.

Under such conditions, my need of the assistance of many in defending this little work now completed is in exact proportion to my lack of native ability for the task at its inception. For as I was both young in years and not much advanced in learning, I did not have the

13

courage to make known my intention by consulting any of the learned, for fear that they would put a stop to my work because of its crudeness of style.

Unknown to others and secretly, so to speak, I worked alone. Sometimes I composed with great effort, again I destroyed what I had poorly written; and thus I strove according to may ability, scarcely adequate though that was, none the less to complete a composition from the thoughts in the writing with which I had become acquainted within the confines of our monastery at Gandersheim: first through the instructive guidance of our learned and kindly teacher Rikkardis, and of others who taught in her stead; and then through the gracious considerations of the royal Gerberga, under whose rule as Abbess I am living at present. Though she is younger in years than I am, yet, as befits a niece of the Emperor, she is farther advanced in learning, and she it was who right kindly instructed me in those various authors whom she herself studied under the guidance of learned teachers.

Even though the art of prosody may seem difficult and arduous for one of my feeble sex, nevertheless, relying in my own strength, I have attempted to sing the songs of this little collection in the dactylic strains, solicitous that the slight talent of ability given me by Heaven should not lie idle in the dark recesses of the mind and thus be destroyed by the rust of neglect, I submitted it under the mallet of ready devotion, so that thus it might sound some little cord of Divine praise. Thus, though I had not the opportunity to achieve any other gain through use of that talent, it might at least be transformed into an instrument of value at the end.

Wherefore, gentle reader, whosoever thou mayest be, if thou art truly wise before God, do not hesitate to lend the assistance of thy correcting power to the poor page which lacks the skill of a master hand. If, however, thou findest something which is worthy of approval, give credit to God for this success and at the same time ascribe all the blemishes to my lack of care.

Let this be done, not in a spirit of censure, but of kindliness; for the keen edge of censure is blunted when it encounters the humility of self-depreciation.

Then Hroswitha addresses her Abbess.

Dedication to Gerberga: Hail, illustrious offspring of a royal race! Gerberga, renowned for thy character and thy learning. Fostering Mistress, do thou accept with kindly mien these little verses which I offer for thy correction, and do thou graciously direct the crude measures of her whom thine excellent precepts instruct. And when thou art indeed wearied with thy manifold labors, do thou deign to recreate thyself in the conning of these measures, and attempt to purify the unlovely muse and to uphold her by the prestige of thine office.

Thus may the zeal of the pupil enhance the praise of the mistress, and the poems of the devoted disciple, the praise of the teacher.

The Eight Sacred Legends

Hroswitha used poetic freedom in the psychological treatment of her characters and their actions. Her writings are varied in subject and are filled with miracles. The first poem, *Maria*, she tells us, was taken from the *Apocryphal Gospel of Saint James* and is in honor of the Virgin Mary. After an impassioned appeal to the "Illustrious Mother of the King, the resplendent Star of the Sea," Hroswitha tells with humble piety of the miraculous birth of the Virgin, her marriage, the Birth of the Christ-child, and their flight into Egypt. This is followed by a short but tender narrative of *The Ascension of our Lord*, translated, she says, by John the Bishop from Greek into Latin. She ends with the appeal, "May he whoever reads these lines, say with a pitying heart: Gentle King, have mercy on poor Hroswitha and spare her, and grant that she may with grace from Heaven continue to sing Thy Divine praises, who in verse has set forth Thy Marvels."

Her third legend, drawn from the store of marvelous narratives from which *The Acts of the Saints* were assembled, tells of Gongolf, a Frankish leader in the Merovingian age in France, who won all hearts by his beauty and godliness. His beautiful but faithless wife plotted against him with a lover of low descent who murdered the saint, and the guilty ones fled. However, divine justice follows swiftly. By heaven's decree the murderer "poured out bowels and heart, so lately puffed with pride and sin," and when the wicked consort vents her scorn upon the pilgrims at the wonder-working tomb of the martyr, she is condemned to bring forth loathsome sounds "so that she, who had refused to maintain due chastity, was a source of uncontrolled ridicule to all."

It will be seen that some of those whom Hroswitha calls "saints" are not saints of the Church, but saints in the sense used by Saint Paul in his Epistle to the Romans, in which he calls all Christians "Saints."

The next poem deals with a more recent martyr, the Spanish youth Pelagius, who fell victim to a lecherous Moorish despot. Hroswitha said that she had heard the story from a visitor from Cordova who had been an eyewitness, hence the realistic description. When the Christian youth repelled the Mohammedan ruler, he was condemned to death; his execution was attended by a series of miracles. Pelagius was hurled by a catapult high over the walls of the city, and fell upon the rocks unharmed. He was then beheaded, "while his soul soars aloft to realms of celestial glory where no words of piety can describe the gleam of his laurel crown, coruscant with the chastity which he had so well maintained."

The Fall and Conversion of Theophilus is the last poem in this group. It is based on the old Greek story of a bond with the Devil whereby earthly joys are given in return for eternal damnation. Theophilus was the first of the medieval figures to become the hero of this theme—one which was repeated in succeeding years down to Goethe's *Faust*. Jealousy and ambition drove him to accept the aid of the Evil One, but God did not desert the recreant soul in whose heart good blazed into penitence. The Holy Virgin yielded to his prayers and forced the Devil to return the contract. Hroswitha's penetration of the agonies he suffered in his final ascent to sanctity is most touching.

Hroswitha dedicated the last three of the eight poems to her beloved Abbess: "Behold, I bring to thee, Gerberga, my Lady, new verses, thus adding songs to the songs I have been commissioned to write; and how a wretched sinner won loving forgiveness, I joyfully sing in dactylic strains; do not choose to spurn these, even though they be exceedingly crude, but do thou praise with gentle heart the works of God."

The first poem in this group, *Basilius*, has again the Faustian theme of the conflict between good and evil. A rich man of Caesarea, wishing to save the soul of his only daughter whom he loved with deep affection, "planned to associate her with the holy maidens who were consecrated to Christ by the sacred veil of virginity and protected in the narrow enclosure of the monastery." However, her servant conceived a passion for her and appealed to the Devil, who planted a reciprocal passion in the breast of the innocent maiden. Hroswitha understands well the human frailties of the world and unravels the plot with great dexterity, and good triumphs over evil.

The seventh legend was altered from an old *Vita* and tells the vivid story of Dionysius of Athens, said to have been converted by Saint Paul and "subsequently chosen bishop of a Christian flock." The Pope sent him to Paris to convert the Gauls and a struggle ensued between paganism and Christianity, "but the fierce deceit of the ancient serpent raged thereupon in indignation that he should now lose so many souls which he had previously been holding captive in the bitter snares of error." Consequently Dionysius was beheaded.

17

"Then the headless trunk of the dead pontiff raised itself in calm beauty, and lifting its own head in its strong arms—and passing over the tedious distance of two miles—it came to a spot fit for the preservation of that body."

In the last of the poems, Agnes, "a virgin who, desiring to despise the empty vanities of a perishable world and the luxury of the frail flesh," suffered martyrdom in defense of her virginity. Hroswitha tells in a most worldly fashion of how Agnes, having refused the offer of marriage from a pagan youth, was "deprived of her garments and with body entirely exposed to be dragged in the midst of a great concourse of people that had gathered, and to be shut up in the dark den of a brothel, in which wanton youths, maddened with passion, delighted in association with evil women. But Christ bringing consolation to His own spouse, did not suffer her to be touched by any one of these revelers. For when she was thus exposed—immediately the luxuriant hair, which hung in loose tresses—grew longer, and in its descent reached the tender soles of her feet so that her entire body was covered." She was condemned to be burned, but when the flames failed to burn her, she was slain with a sword, and an angel bore her soul aloft with celestial splendor, while she waved farewell to her parents.

In a brief note placed between the legends and the plays, Hroswitha speaks of her sources: "I found all the material I have used in this book in various ancient works by authors of reputation, with the exception of the story of the martyrdom of St. Pelagius, which has been told here in verse. The details of this were supplied to me by an inhabitant of the town where the Saint was put to death. This truthful stranger assured me that he had not only seen Pelagius, whom he described as the most beautiful of men, face to face, but had been a witness of his end. If anything has crept into my other compositions, the accuracy of which can be challenged, it is not my fault, unless it be a fault to have reproduced the statements of unreliable authorities."

The Six Rhymed Dramas

Hroswitha's six short dramas in rhymed prose are considered her most important and original contribution to literature. They are certainly the best known of her works, as they have been produced on the stage from time to time with success (see list of performances, p. 35). They have been proved theatrically practical, the dialogue is lively and at times stirring, and the structure has continuity. It is not known if the plays were ever produced during the lifetime of Hroswitha, but she must have written them with that purpose in mind, as a few stage directions are found attached to *Gallicanus* and *Calimachus* in the *Munich Codex*. These were later omitted by Celtes in the first printed edition of her works in 1501. As silence was required during mealtime in the refectory, when sacred scriptures, legends, and the early classics were read aloud, it is quite possible that the plays were read, as well. Thus, they may have become familiar to the canonesses.

Sister Mary Marguerite Butler says: "There are strong evidences of three contemporary dramatic streams within Hroswitha's writings—the literary tradition of classical antiquity, the mimetic influence, and the liturgical form—and the traces of their concomitant theatrical characteristics." Hroswitha followed the structure of the plays of the pagan poet Terence, but, as a devout Christian, wrote from an entirely different point of view. She showed great skill in the development of her characters.

In the plays, Hroswitha treated sensual passion in an even

19

more realistic manner than in her first poems, but with the same delicacy of feeling and sincere simplicity. Although she believed that chastity was the crowning glory of a perfect life, she did not condemn marriage; in speaking of Henry the Fowler she says: "With him ruled his illustrious wife, Mathilda, who now, in all the realm none will be found to surpass in exalted holiness. Their union the triune God blessed with three sons." Hroswitha even shows a certain amount of sympathy for those who err, and treats her characters as human beings with all their faults and virtues, but inspired by a spark of sacred fire. She could not resist pointing a moral in each play.

Protestations of modesty and excuses for lack of skill were customary in the writings of Hroswitha's day. There is no doubt but that she was genuinely modest about her work, and always gave credit to her teachers and especially gave thanks repeatedly "for any talent I may have—given me by the merciful grace of Heaven in which I have trusted, rather than to my own strength." However, it may be seen in the following prefaces that with increasing experience she gained confidence in herself, had a surer touch, and explained her purpose very clearly.

The plays and prefaces are in the translation of Christopher St. John (pseudonym for Christabel Marshall), *The Plays of Hroswitha*, London, 1923:

Preface to the Plays of Hroswitha, German Religious and Virgin of the Saxon Race:

There are many Catholics, and we cannot entirely acquit ourselves of the charge, who, attracted by the polished elegance of the style of pagan writers, prefer their works to the holy scriptures. There are others who, although they are deeply attached to the sacred writings and have no liking for most pagan productions, make an exception in favor of the works of Terence, and, fascinated by the charm of the manner, risk being corrupted by the wickedness of the matter. Wherefore I, the strong voice of Gandersheim, have not hesitated to imitate in my writings a poet whose works are so widely read, my object being to glorify within the limits of my poor talent, the laudable chastity of Christian virgins in that self-same form of composition which has been used to describe the shameless acts of licentious women. One thing has all the same embarrassed me and often brought a blush to my cheek. It is that I have been compelled through the nature of this work to apply my mind and my pen to depicting the dreadful frenzy of those possessed by unlawful love, and the insidious sweetness of passion-things which should not even be named among us. Yet, if from modesty, I had refrained from treating these subjects, I should not have been able to attain my object—to glorify the innocent to the best of my ability. For the more seductive the blandishments of lovers, the more wonderful the divine succor, and the greater the merit of those who resist, especially when it is fragile woman who is victorious and strong man who is routed with confusion.

I have no doubt that many will say that my poor work is much inferior to that of the author whom I have taken as my model, that it is on a much humbler scale, and indeed altogether different.

Well, I do not deny this. None can justly accuse me of wishing to place myself on a level with those who by the sublimity of their genius have so far outstripped me. No, I am not so arrogant as to compare myself even with the least among the scholars of the ancient world. I strive only, although my power is not equal to my desire, to use what talent I have for the glory of Him Who gave it to me. Nor is my self-love so great that I would, to avoid criticism, abstain from proclaiming wherever possible the virtues of Christ working in His saints. If this pious devotion gives satisfaction I shall rejoice, if it does not, either on account of my own worthlessness or of the faults of my unpolished style, I shall still be glad that I made the effort.

In the humbler works of my salad days I gathered up my poor researches in heroic strophes, but here I have sifted them into a series of dramatic scenes and avoided through omission the pernicious voluptuousness of pagan writers.

The Abbess Gerberga took great pride in the writings of her friend and pupil, Hroswitha, and brought them to the attention of the scholars who visited the monastery, especially to the Archbishop William of Mainz, the illegitimate son of Otto I, and to her sympathetic young friend, Otto II. (Later Hroswitha was to write the life of the Ottos at the request of Gerberga.)

The second preface is addressed to her readers, "Epistle of the Same to Certain Learned Patrons of this Book":

To you, learned and virtuous men, who do not envy the success of others, but on the contrary rejoice in it as becomes the truly great, Hroswitha, poor humble sinner, sends wishes for your health in this life and your joy in eternity.

I cannot praise you enough for your humility or pay an adequate tribute to your kindness and affection. To think that you, who have been nurtured in the most profound philosophical studies, and have attained knowledge in perfection, should have deigned to approve the humble work of an obscure woman! You have, however, not praised me but the Giver of the grace which works in me, by sending me your paternal congratulations and admitting that I possess some little knowledge of those arts the subtleties of which exceed the grasp of my woman's mind. Until I showed my work to you I had not dared to let anyone see it except my intimate companions. I came near abandoning this form of writing altogether, for if there were few to whom I could submit my compositions at all there were fewer still who could point out what needs correction and encourage me to go on. But now, reassured by your verdict (is it not said that the testimony of three witnesses is "equivalent to the truth?"), I feel that I have enough confidence to apply myself to writing, if God grants me the power, and that I need not fear the criticism of the learned whoever they may be. Still, I am torn by conflicting feelings. I rejoice from the depths of my soul that God through Whose grace alone I am what I am should be praised in me, but I am afraid of being thought greater than I am. I know that it is as wrong to deny a divine gift as to pretend falsely that we have received it. So I will not deny that through the grace of the Creator I have acquired some knowledge of the arts. He has given me the ability to learn—I am a teachable creature—yet of myself I should know nothing. He has given me a perspicacious mind, but one that lies fallow and idle when it is not cultivated. That my natural gifts might not be made void by negligence I have been at pains, whenever I have been able to pick up some threads and scraps torn from the old mantle of philosophy, to weave them into the stuff of my own book, in the hope that my lowly ignorant effort may gain more acceptance through the introduction of something of a nobler strain, and that the Creator of genius may be the more honored since it is generally believed that a woman's intelligence is slower. Such has been my motive in writing, the sole reason for the sweat and fatigue which my labors have cost me. At least I do not pretend to have knowledge where I am ignorant. On the contrary, my best claim to indulgence is that I know how much I do not know.

Impelled by your kindly interest and your express wish I come bowing low like a reed, to submit this little work to your judgment. I wrote it indeed with that idea in my mind, although doubt as to its merits had made me withhold it until now. I hope you will revise it with the same careful attention that you would give to a work of your own, and that when you have succeeded in bringing it up to the proper standard you will return it to me, that I may learn what are its worst faults.

The Arguments to the Plays

Sister Mary Marguerite Butler has pointed to the variety of moods—tragic, comic, heroic, romantic, and didactic—to be found in the "Arguments" written by Hroswitha for each play. However, short additional notes have been included here with the hope of further clarifying the plots of these extraordinary dramas.

Argument to the play *Gallicanus*: The conversion of Gallicanus, Commander-in-Chief. On the eve of his departure for a campaign

23

against the Scythians, Gallicanus is bethrothed to the Emperor Constantine's daughter, Constance, a consecrated Virgin.

When threatened with defeat in battle, Gallicanus is converted by John and Paul, Grand Almoners to Constance. He is immediately baptized and takes a vow of celibacy.

Later he is exiled by order of Julian the Apostate, and receives the crown of martyrdom. John and Paul are put to death by the same prince and buried secretly in their own house. Not long after, the son of their executioner becomes possessed by a devil. He is cured after confessing the crime committed by his father. He bears witness to the merits of the martyrs, and is baptized, together with his father.

NOTE: Constance was a thoughtful young princess, for as a consecreted virgin she knew that she would never marry Gallicanus, but as his going to battle depended upon her consent, and as she realized that the success of the campaign rested upon him, she consented, prayed, and played for time. In the absence of the General she converted his two daughters to Christianity, and relied upon the strategy of John and Paul to convert Gallicanus, which was accomplished amid miraculous manifestations from heaven, and the day was saved.

Argument to the play *Dulcitius*: The martyrdom of the holy virgins Agape, Chionia, and Irena. The Governor Dulcitius seeks them out in the silence of the night with criminal intent, but hardly has he entered their dwelling than he becomes the victim of a delusion, under which he mistakes for the objects of his passion the saucepans and frying-pans in the kitchen. These he embraces and covers with kisses until his face and clothes are black with soot and dirt. Later, by order of Diocletian, he hands the maidens over to the care of Sisinnius, who is charged with their punishment. Sisinnius in his turn is made the sport of the most strange delusions, but at length succeeds in getting Agape and Chionia burnt, Irena shot to death with arrows.

NOTE: The plays of Hroswitha have been called comedies, but it seems that the only real comedy, in the modern sense of the word, is that of *Dulcitius*, where humor and gravity are strangely combined and the situations are truly ludicrous. In this play, fragile woman is victorious and strong man is routed with confusion, for the predicament of Dulcitius when he emerged from his encounter with the pots and pans was most humiliating. When the Christian maidens refused to worship the Roman gods and marry pagans they were sentenced to be burned. However, Agape appealed for divine aid saying: "O Lord, we know Thy power! It would not be anything strange or new if the fire forgot its nature and obeyed thee. But we are weary of this world, and we implore thee to break the bonds that chain our souls, and to let our bodies be consumed that we may rejoice with thee in heaven." The soldiers exclaimed: "O most wonderful! Their spirits have left their bodies, but there is no sign of any hurt."

Argument to the play *Calimachus*: The resurrection of Drusiana and Calimachus.

Calimachus cherishes a guilty passion for Drusiana, not only while she is alive but after she has died in the Lord. He dies from the bite of a serpent but, thanks to the prayers of St. John the Apostle, he is restored to life, together with Drusiana, and is born again in Christ.

NOTE: With the connivance of an unscrupulous servant, Calimachus visited the tomb where he found Drusiana's body looking more beautiful than in life. When about to embrace her, he was miraculously saved from the sacrilege by a serpent. It is an extraordinary plot to have been chosen from a classical source by a cloistered canoness, but it is delicately and skillfully handled.

Argument to the play *Abraham*: The fall and repentance of Mary, the niece of the hermit Abraham, who, after she had spent twenty years in the religious life as a solitary, abandons it in despair, and returning to the world, does not shrink from becoming a harlot. But two years later Abraham, in the disguise of a lover, seeks her out and reclaims her. For twenty years she does penance for her sins with many tears, fastings, vigils, and prayers.

NOTE: Mary only abandoned her religious life after being seduced by a false monk. The scene between Abraham and Mary in the brothel is compassionate and dramatic, and the play has been considered a masterpiece. When Mary hears her uncle's pleas to return to a life of virtue she cries that everything is over for her, but he assures her that "it is human to sin"—"but it is devilish to continue to sin." When she returns to the desert she prays for the men who are tempted to sin through her.

Argument to the play *Paphnutius*: The conversion of Thaïs by the hermit Paphnutius. Obedient to a vision, he leaves the desert and, disguised as a lover, seeks out Thaïs in Alexandria. She is moved to repent by his exhortations and, renouncing her evil life, consents to be enclosed in a narrow cell, where she does penance for three years. Paphnutius learns from a vision granted to St. Anthony's disciple Paul that her humility has won her a place among the blessed in Paradise. He brings her out of her cell and stays by her side until her soul has left her body.

NOTE: The story is preceded by a learned philosophical discourse between Paphnutius and his disciples. He explains in terms of music the "harmonious arrangement"—"between the mortal body and the spiritual soul." He also gives a technical explanation of the three kinds of music: human, celestial, and from instruments as belonging to "one of the branches of the Quadrivium."

Argument to the play *Sapientia*: The martyrdom of the holy virgins Faith, Hope, and Charity, who are put to the torture by the Emperor Hadrian and slain in the presence of their mother, Sapientia, she encouraging them by her admonitions to bear their sufferings. After their death the holy mother recovers the bodies of her children, embalms them in spices, and buries them with honor about five miles outside the city of Rome.

Forty days later the spirit of Sapientia takes its flight to heaven while she is still praying by her children's grave.

NOTE: This play has been considered by dramatists the least successful, and is historically incorrect, as Hadrian was known to be tolerant toward Christians. When the Emperor asks Sapientia the ages of her children, she replies with a numerical discourse on the science of numbers, hoping to confound him, but failing. Christopher St. John thinks that Hroswitha introduced the scientific discussion to impress "the learned men to whom she submitted her work," because it throws an interesting light on the studies pursued in a monastery in the tenth century.

The Achievements of Otto

Hroswitha's two historical epics, the *Carmen de Gestis Oddonis*, also called *Gesta Ottonis* or *Panegyric Oddonum*, and the *Primordia Coenobii Gandeshemensis*, are closely allied. They were both translated with their prefaces by Sister Mary Bernardine Bergman, A.B., A.M., from the German text of the Teubner edition of Karl Strecker, *Hrotsvithae Opera*, with such minor changes as she has noted in her introduction; it is the only text in English.

The *Gesta Ottonis* starts with the "just and wise reign of Henry the Fowler, first King of Saxony," but is primarily a panegyric of the deeds of the Emperor Otto I, called the Great, and Otto II, who ruled jointly with his father from the age of six. Sister Mary Marguerite Butler says that the *Hildesheim Chronical* states that Hroswitha originally honored the three

Ottos, and that the very title of this book, *Panegyric Oddonum*, known as the *Gesta Ottonis*, proves that we have only the first part; she thinks that the second dedication, addressed to Otto II, probably served as the preface to a second book, which is lost. The epic consists of 1517 verses, of which 676 lines are unfortunately missing. The *Gesta Ottonis* ends with the marriage of Liudolf, Duke of Swabia, when Otto I was at the height of his power; this topic Hroswitha feared to treat because "I am withheld by my womanly nature—hence I, hindered by the weightiness of these great themes, proceed no further, but prudently make an end."

The *Gesta Ottonis* is prized by historians, who have found it a valuable account of the period although it is at times inaccurate because of omissions and alterations made for diplomatic reasons. Hroswitha found the writing of political facts very difficult, as will be seen in the address to Gerberga and in the dedications to Otto I and Otto II, which precede the poem. It was hard to write the truth about living people, especially during civil war when the members of the Saxon royal family were literally at sword's point. The most treacherous offenders against Otto I were Prince Liudolf, who plotted against his father, and Duke Henry of Bavaria, brother of the King and father of Abbess Gerberga, who had requested Hroswitha to write the *Gesta Ottonis*. This created a delicate situation because of Hroswitha's close association with the family, so she tactfully blamed their misdeeds on "the wicked cunning of the ancient foe" who "disturbed our placid existence by his ancient wiles"—"which always seeks to pervert feeble hearts, did not cease, but after the deed of ill urged the addition of a worse crime. The Enemy is said to have entered the breasts of certain men with such frenzy of destructive poison that they desired to inflict death upon the faithful King

28

and to appoint his brother as ruler over the nation—but the Paschal Lamb, who gave Himself in death as a chosen holocaust to His Father for our redemption, permitted not the commission of that hideous crime. But presently, he exposed their plan to all men, and thus happily the blood of the innocent King was saved, and those who were found guilty of the accursed crime were condemned to bitter punishment in proportion of the measure of their guilt."

With all this and more to contend with, it is no wonder that she cries, "I do not think it fitting for a frail woman abiding in the enclosure of a peaceful monastery to speak of war, with which she ought not even to be acquainted. These matters should be reserved for the toil of qualified men, to whom wisdom of mind has granted the ability to express all things wisely in eloquent terms."

Hroswitha's dedication to Gerberga, therefore, should be read with an understanding of the political and personal considerations that influenced it:

To Gerberga, renowned Abbess, esteemed no less for her integrity than for her illustrious descent from a royal race. I, Hrotsvit of Gandersheim, the lowest of the lowly of those serving under the sway of her ladyship, wish to offer all that a servant owes to her mistress.

O my mistress, thou who enlightenest by the radiant diversity of thy spiritual wisdom, may it not irk thy kindliness to examine carefully what thou knowest has been written at thy bidding.

Thou hast indeed imposed upon me the difficult task of narrating in verse the achievements of an august emperor, which thou art well aware was impossible to gather abundantly from hearsay. Thou canst surmise what great difficulties my ignorance puts in my way while engaged in this work. There are things of which I could find no written record, nor could I elicit information from anyone sufficiently reliable. I was like a stranger wandering without a guide through the

29

depth of an unknown forest where every path was covered over and mantled with heavy snow. In vain he tries to follow the directions of those who are showing the way only by a nod. Now he wanders through pathless ways, now by chance he comes upon the trail of the right path, until at length, when he has traversed half of the thick-treed domain, he attains the place of long-sought rest. There staying his step, he dares not proceed farther, until either he is led on by someone overtaking him or follows the footsteps of one who has preceded him. In like manner, I, bidden to undertake a complete chronicle of illustrious achievements, have gone on my way stumbling and hesitating, so great was the difficulty of finding a path in the forest of these royal deeds.

And so, wearied by my endeavor, I have lapsed into silence as I pause in a convenient resting place. Without guidance I propose to go no further. If, however, I be encouraged by the eloquent treatises of the learned (either already written or in the near future to be written) I might perhaps discover the means of veiling to some degree my homely simplicity.

Now, however, in proportion as I am unsupported by any authority, I am defenseless at every point. I fear, too, that I shall be accused of temerity and that I shall encounter the reproaches of many, because I have dared to disgrace by my uncultured style matters that should be set forth with the festal eloquence of choice expression. Yet, if a person of good judgment, who knows how to appraise things fairly, examines my work, he will pardon me the more readily because of the weakness of my sex and the inferiority of my knowledge, especially since I undertook this little work not of my own presumption, but at thy bidding.

Why, then, should I fear the criticism of others, since, if I have erred somewhat, I become responsible only to your judgment? O, why can I not escape reproofs for these works about which I was anxious to be silent? If, because of its crudeness, I should wish the work to be shown to none, should I not deserve the blame of all? To your decision, however, and that of your most intimate friend, Archbishop William, to whom you have bidden me present this testimony of my simplicity, I submit the work to be appraised for its worth and its imperfections.

The following is Hroswitha's dedication to Otto I; the remarks above concerning the author's relationship to the various members of the royal family should be borne in mind.

Otto, mighty sovereign of the empire of the Caesars, who, renowned because thou wieldest a sceptre of imperial majesty by the indulgent kindliness of the Eternal King, surpassest in integrity all foregoing emperors, many nations dwelling far and wide reverence thee; the Roman Empire, too, bestows upon thee manifold honors! Do not reject the small offerings of this poem, but may this proffered tribute of praises which the least of the flock of Gandersheim accords thee be pleasing. The kind solicitude of thy forbears has assembled it, and the constant desire of rendering service owes it to thee. Many, perchance, have written and many hereafter will produce masterful memorials of thy achievements. But none of these has provided a model for me, nor have monographs, hitherto written, taught me what I should set down. But devotedness of heart alone is the reason for this undertaking, and this urged me to dare the formidable task. Yet, I am fearful that by verse I may be heedlessly tracing spurious deeds of thine and not disclosing authentic ones. But no baneful presumption of mind has urged me in this matter, nor have I voluntarily played falsely by a disdain of the truth as a whole. But, that the account, as I have written it, is true, those who furnished the material for me themselves declared. Let not, therefore, the benignity of august majesty despise that which a lowly suppliant, devoted of heart, has achieved. And, although hereafter many books may be written praising thee duly, and may be esteemed fittingly acceptable to thee, yet, let this little book which has clearly been written from no earlier copy be not the last in order of regard. And, although thou holdest the honor of Caesar's emperorship, disdain not to be called by the name of King, until, the fame of a royal life having been written, the imperial splendor of the second realm may be declared in an orderly fashion and in becoming language.

Hroswitha's dedication to his son, Otto II, then follows:

Otto, resplendent ornament of the Roman Empire, bright scion of the august and revered Otto, for whom the mighty King throned

31

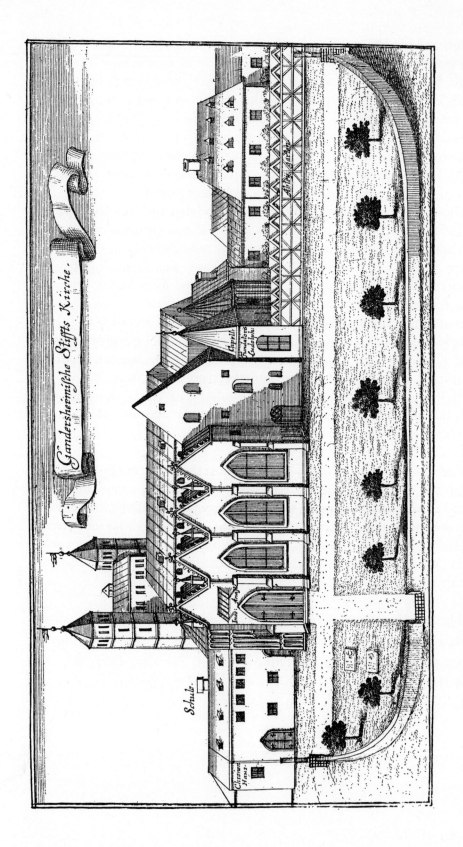

Gandersheim Cloister Church. Engraved plate from Johann Georg Leuckfeld, *Antiquitates Gandersheimenses*, Wolfenbüttel, 1709.

on high and his Eternal Son destined an empire strong in the zenith of its power: spurn not the poor composition of a poor nun! Thou, thyself, if thou deign to remember, hast lately ordered it to be presented to thy keen gaze; and when thou perceivest that it is marred with many blemishes, be then the more inclined to favor a speedy pardon, the more I am but obeying thy behest in presenting it to thee. If I were not urged by thy dread command, under no circumstance, should I have such self-assurance as to presume to offer to thy scrutiny this little book with its obvious lack of polish.

Thou, who by the decree of God art associated with thy father in his court and art ready to obey his paternal admonitions, holdest harmoniously a like distinction of imperial rule, bearing the kingly sceptre in thy youthful hands. But, since I know that thou art loftily considered like to Solomon, son of the celebrated King David, who, in his father's presence and at his revered command, received the paternal kingdom amid desired peace, I hope that in accord with his example thou wilt be content. Though Solomon, as king resided in a proud citadel, wisely establishing the decrees of sacred laws and penetrating with profound mind into the secrets of nature, yet occasionally he was disposed to relax his mind with trivial investigations. But he did not loathe duly to settle, with the determination of a just and speedy decision, the quarrel of the two women, ordering the child to be restored to its true mother.

Therefore, as a suppliant indeed, I request that thou, our Solomon, though the administration of a harassing empire occupy thee, deign to read now, for amusement, the recent account of thine own poor nun; that thus all crudeness of utterance, in this treatise on thy imperial name, may presently disappear from the badly arranged words, and that enhanced by thy revered title, they may be guarded from the breath of well-merited contempt.

The writing of the *Primordia Coenobii Gandeshemensis* was a labor of love for Hroswitha, as it recounts the founding of Gandersheim in 856 by Duke Liudolf, his wife Oda, who lived there beloved by all to the age of 107, and her mother Aeda. Hroswitha tells of the completion of the monastery by

Liudolf's son, Otto the Illustrious, and the reign of his daughters, who were the first three Abbesses. The subject was close to her heart and she wove many spiritual legends into the history with skill and charm, and the miracles which occurred during the building were all very real to her. They were written in much the same manner that Wagner used to weave the legend of Lohengrin around the historic figure of Henry the Fowler, father of Otto I.

If it is true that Hroswitha was born about 935 and entered the cloister about 955, she would have been sixty-five years of age when she died, having spent forty-five wonderful years in study and creative writing.

Otto III, a strong Grecophile, died unmarried in Rome. He, the Abbess Gerberga, and Hroswitha probably all died within a few months of each other during 1001–1002, and it must have been a great sorrow to the bereaved. Otto II had given his five-year-old daughter Sophia to Gerberga to be educated at Gandersheim, so now after some years as a canoness she was consecrated Abbess. This marked the end of an era; the rule of the three Ottos was over, and jealous disputes arose among the clergy of the diocese. The literary prestige of the monastery declined, and it was two hundred years after "the strong voice of Gandersheim" was stilled before another medieval dramatist appeared.

Performances of Hroswitha's Plays

MARJORIE DANA BARLOW

The following list of the theatrical performances of the plays of Hroswitha has been collected for this book because the one subject which is so often discussed and argued over in writing about the poet is whether the plays were ever acted during her lifetime. Not wishing to add anything further to the many speculations and conjectures already published on the subject, we have gathered a tentative list of the performances of her plays which we know to have been given. As we go to press, reports are still coming in from a number of sources indicating that there have been many more performances than we have been able to authentically include here. Information for entries marked with an asterisk (*) was taken from Bert Nagel, Hrotsvit von Gandersheim, Stuttgart, 1965, pp. 76–78. A dagger (†) indicates performances reported to us by Eduard Brodführer of Bad Gandersheim/Harz, Germany.

c. 1888–1889. *Abraham* and *Paphnutius* were performed by the marionettes of M. Signoret at the Galerie Vivienne, Rue Vivienne, Paris, at the suggestion of Anatole France in *Le Temps*, June 10, 1888. His article in *Le Temps*, April 7, 1889, records the performances.

1900. *Dulcitius*. The German Lyceum-Club of Berlin, an organization of literature- and art-loving women, performed a superbly effective production of the play (according to Paul von Winterfeld).*

1914, January 11–12. *Paphnutius* in English was produced at the Savoy Theater by the Pioneer Players, London, with Ellen Terry as

35

the Nun. Christopher St. John (pseudonym for Christabel Marshall) translated the text for this production; she also served as advisor for the stage presentation. Edith Craig directed the performances on consecutive nights. Though apparently originally scheduled for King's Hall, Covent Garden, the play actually appeared at the Savoy.

1920, December 20. *Calimachus* in English. The Art Theater, London, put the play on for a matinee, using a translation of Arthur Waley, Assistant Curator of Prints at the British Museum. The Art Theater had offices at 43 Russell Square, London; its Trustees were Lord Howard de Walden and S. Lee Masters; its Director was Mme. Bonnet; and the Honorary Secretary was Mrs. H. M. Adler.

c. 1922–1923. *Calimachus* in Latin was performed at the University of Edinburgh, Scotland, in about 1922. (Reported by E. Amsell, Deputy Librarian, University Library, Cambridge, England.)

1924, January. *Paphnutius* in English. Under the direction of Mr. Nugent Monck, the play was performed at the Maddermarket Theater in conjunction with a lecture. The script of the play was taken from H. J. W. Tillyard's English translation in *The Plays of Roswitha*, London, 1923.

1926, April 5–11. *Abraham, Calimachus,* and *Dulcitius* in English, were presented at the Lawren Theater Studio, New York, "under the sensitive and imaginative direction of Wladimir Nelidoff" quoted from the play program. The translation was probably that of Christopher St. John. Joseph Lawren was a producer in New York.

1926, June 13. *Calimachus and Dulcitius.* During the Hroswitha Festival in Bad Gandersheim, "Die Erweckung des Calimachus" [*Calimachus*] and *Dulcitius* were performed on June 13th, under the revision of Else Schulhoff of Berlin. The revision was based on the translation of Bendixen. The play was directed by Oberstudienrat Karl Tägtmeyer, who is well deserving of Hroswitha scholarship. The reviews of these performances were generally favorable, but did not lack some censure.†

1926, December. "The London Roswitha Society is in the process of selecting works from their patroness, Roswitha of Gandersheim, works that with a few cuts will also find favor in our own time." (Cited from the *Osservatore Romano*, December 3, 1926.)*

1927. *Abraham* and *Dulcitius* were performed in the Hanover Municipal Theater. The revision was by L. Stahl.*

1927, September 27–29. *Abraham* and *Dulcitius*. At the Convention of German Philologists, Pedagogues, and High School Teachers in Göttingen, Germany, Dr. Roennecke, Director of the Stadttheater in Göttingen, produced Hroswitha's "Südenfall und Umkehr der Klausnerin Maria" (The Fall and Conversion of the Recluse Maria) [*Abraham*], and *Dulcitius*, in the second revision of Leopold Stahl. The introductory lecture, "Why do we go to the theater and what do we search there?" was given by Professor Friedrich Neumann. The excellent performance did not make a lasting impression on the audience.†

1928. *Abraham*. The Munich Calderon-Institute performed "Heimkehr einer Verirrten" (The Return of the Confused One) [*Abraham*] in Gandersheim. The criticism was unfavorable.*

1928. *Paphnutius*. A student production of "Thais" [Paphnutius] was given in Gandersheim on the occasion of the fiftieth anniversary of the Gymnasium.

1928, April 15. *Abraham* in German was presented at the Altonaer Stadttheater, Hamburg-Altona, Germany. Dr. Carl Brinitzer adapted the play, giving it not a literal translation, but a free rendition of his own. He was at the time an undergraduate. In the cast was Gustav Knuth, one of Germany's best actors.

1928, July. *Abraham*. A repeat performance of the Altonaer Stadttheater production of Carl Brinitzer was given in Munich.*

1928. *Abraham* and *Dulcitius* were performed as the medieval plays of the annual Dürer celebration in Nürnberg during the summer of 1928.

1930, February. *Paphnutius* in English was produced at the Yale Drama School as a thesis production of Andrina McIntyre (M.F.A., 1934). The translation was that of Christopher St. John. The production book includes an essay and bibliography.

1930, February 9. *Paphnutius*. On February 9, 1930, Gandersheim organized a Hroswitha Day. At 12:15 in the afternoon, the "creative women" (Die schaffenden Frauen) assembled at a Radio Convention to hear the world premiere of the Funksuite "Thais" from themes of Hroswitha's "Bekehrung der Buhlerin Thais" (The Conversion of the Courtesan Thais) [*Paphnutius*], revised by Alice Fliegel and put to music by Gerhard Maas. First movement: "Der Einsiedler" (The Hermit); second movement: "Sünde" (Sin); third movement: "Bekehrung" (Conversion); and Finale. The Hroswitha Day had a tremendous response in Germany and abroad. The *Kriesblatt* of Gandersheim lists numerous reports not only from Germany but also from England, Turkey, and America.†

1930. *Paphnutius*. On the occasion of a Hroswitha Evening of the Stadtische Volkshochschule in Halberstadt, Germany, the Funksuite "Thais" [*Paphnutius*], which had had its premiere on February 9th of 1930 in Bad Gandersheim, was repeated.†

1933. *Abraham* and *Paphnutius*. During the Heimfestspiele in 1933, "Die Busse der Maria" (The Repentance of Maria) was performed. This was a stage revision by Else Schulhoff of Hroswitha's two plays "Fall und Busse der Maria" (The Fall and Repentance of Maria) [*Abraham*] and the "Bekehrung der Thais" (The Conversion of Thais) [*Paphnutius*]. The revision is based on Bendixen's edition. The plot of the first and third acts is staged in Thebes, act two in Alexandria.

1930's. *Abraham* and *Paphnutius*. The German Lyceum-Club of Berlin performed "Die Busse der Maria" (see above, 1933) in the Hroswitha Hall. The stage revision was by Else Schulhoff. It was unanimously applauded. The acting performances, stage setting, lighting, and music fused into an impressive whole.*

1930's. *Calimachus.* Three performances were given in Gandersheim, under the direction of K. Tägtmeyer.*

1934, December 14. *Abraham* in English. The play was performed by the Snarks, a non-professional group of women players, in the chapel of the Church of St. Ignatius Loyola, New York. The *Prologue*, setting the time and place of Hroswitha, was written by Amy Groesbeck and read by Eva McAdoo. The settings were suggested by drawings made from a then uncatalogued eleventh-century Salzburg manuscript in the Morgan Library. The director was Miss Dorothy Sands. The play was accompanied by Gregorian singing by a group from the choir of St. Pius X School. Christopher St. John's translation was used. The *New York Post*, December 17, 1934, praised the "charm, intensity, simplicity and earnestness" of Hroswitha.

1938, April 15. *Gallicanus.* On Good Friday, 1938, the Danish radio broadcasted Hroswitha's "Bekehrung des Feldherrn Gallican" (The Conversion of General Gallican) [Gallicanus], under the direction of Dr. Egil Rostrup.†

1938, April 23. *Gallicanus.* The German Lyceum-Club of Berlin performed the play.*

1939. *Calimachus.* "Le Doigt de Dieu" [*Calimachus*] was produced at the Theatre de l' Oeuvre, 55 rue de Clichy, Paris. The translation was by Raymond Raynal. (Jacques Guignard of the Bibliothèque de l'Arsenal, Paris, supplied this information.)

1943. *Paphnutius* in English. M. O'Shea was head of the Drama Department at Sarah Lawrence College, Bronxville, New York, when the play was performed there. Unfortunately, the present Director of the Performing Arts can give us no further information about this production.

39

1944, November 28. *Abraham* in English was produced at the Cherry Lane Theater, New York, by the Little Theater of St. Therese. This production was written, directed, and produced by Tom Donahue. Leonide Mosa and Eugene Desirio headed the cast.

1950, August 1. *Calimachus* and *Abraham* were presented by the culture association of the Wolfenbüttel Circle in the Kaiser Hall in Gandersheim.*

1950, August 20. *Abraham* in German. In anticipation of the eleven-hundredth anniversary of the foundation of the monastery at Gandersheim, Germany (scheduled for 1952), a group of professional players from Southern Germany, the Calderón-Institute of Munich, was brought up to Gandersheim to enact the play, *Abraham*.

1952, January 31. *Dulcitius*. A student production of Hroswitha's dramatic poetical work *Dulcitius*, translated by George Hauser, was performed in Zurich, Switzerland. The play was directed by Reinhart Spörri.†

1952, April 26. *Dulcitius*. The Zurich production was repeated in Winterthur.*

1952, May 3. *Gallicanus* in Latin was presented by the Classical Department of Bryn Mawr College, Bryn Mawr, Pennsylvania, in honor of Lily Ross Taylor, retiring Dean of the Graduate School, and head of the Classical Department at Bryn Mawr.

1954, April 5. *Paphnutius* in English was produced by Professor F. Theodore Cloak, Chairman of the Department of Drama at Lawrence College, Appelton, Wisconsin, as part of a five-day Medieval Festival, April 4–8, 1954, which was organized and directed by William A. Chaney, Assistant Professor of History and Medievalist at Lawrence College. The play was preceded by a lecture by Professor Cloak, "Performances and Production of Plays in the Middle Ages."

1955, January 15. *Dulcitius* and *Sapientia* in English were performed by the students of Mercy College of Detroit, Michigan, at the Lydia Mendelssohn Theater on the University of Michigan Campus. The production was arranged and directed by Sister Mary Marguerite Butler, R.S.M.

1957. *Dulcitius* and *Sapientia*. In Michigan, Sister Mary Marguerite Butler tested the stageworthiness of both plays on the basis of the research undertaken in Gandersheim itself concerning the possibility of Hroswitha performances in the tenth century. The stage productions, which also strove for authenticity in costume and stage settings, were assisted by the Drama Institute of the University of Michigan, as well as by historians and art historians.*

1962, December. *Abraham* in German. A student production of the play was given in the old assembly hall of the University of Heidelberg. The translation and new revision of the text was by Piltz. The music (a prelude and incidental music) was that of Guillaume de Machaut and Susato. The play was directed by Bernd Rüde.*

1963, February. *Abraham*. The University of Heidelberg production of 1962 was repeated in the framework of a Hroswitha Memorial Hour at the same University. Introductory remarks were given by Bert Nagel. There were very warm responses in the press and on the radio (transmission of selected scenes of the performances). Photographs of the scenes were taken by Nagel.*

ACKNOWLEDGMENTS

I am grateful to the following persons for help in preparing the list of performances of Hroswitha's plays: Sister M. Gonsalva Wiegand, O.S.F., Marian College, Indianapolis, Indiana; Sybil Rosenfeld, Joint Honorary Secretary, Society for Theater Research, 103 Ralph Court, Queensway, London W2, England; Sister M. Xavier Hefner, St. Louis University, St. Louis, Missouri; Sister M. Bernardine Bergman, O.S.B., Benedictine Sisters, Covington, Kentucky.

The Manuscripts

META HARRSEN

1. [All poems, plays, and the chronicle *Gesta Oddonis*]. Munich, Bayerische Staatsbibliothek Clm 14485 (formerly St. Emmeram, Regensburg, E. CVIII).

150 ff., vellum 9½ × 6½ inches, 24 lines, lacuna between ff. 148–149 and 149–150. X and XI century, with initial ornament and rubrics of the XI century.

This is the earliest and most complete text of the works of Hroswitha, containing all the poems: *Maria, Ascensio, Gongolfus, Pelagius, Theophilus, Basilius, Dionysius,* and *Agnes*; all the plays: *Gallicanus, Dulcitius, Calimachus, Abraham, Pafnutius,* and *Sapientia*; the 35-line poem on the *Vision* [*Revelation*] *of St. John* (see below); and the chronicle, *Gesta Oddonis*. It lacks only *Carmen de primordiis et fundatoribus coenobii Gandeshemensis* (hereafter referred to as *Primordia*), and *Vitae paparum SS. Anastasii et Innocentii*, of which there is no extant text (see No. 10).

A short poem of four elegiac distichs, which also appeared in the manuscript, was proved by von Winterfeld to be not by Hroswitha, but a quotation from Bede (see No. 277).

The manuscript is written in a fractured minuscule by several (possibly five) hands, of which the first (ff. 4–19 v) is of the end of the X century. The ductus is vertical, the letters square, and the spacing and alignment are uneven (*Plate 1*).

The last scribe (ff. 80–150) is of the early XI century, as indicated by the occasional use of the uncial form of *d*, and the insufficient

Plate 1. Munich, Bayerische Staatsbibliothek Clm 14485, fol. 3 verso, 4 recto. The beginning of *Maria*. Written in the late tenth century by the first of several scribes who worked on the manuscript.

Plate 2. Munich, Bayerische Staatsbibliothek Clm 14485, fol. 80 verso, 81 recto. The beginning of *Gallicanus*. Written in the early eleventh century by the last scribe who worked on this manuscript.

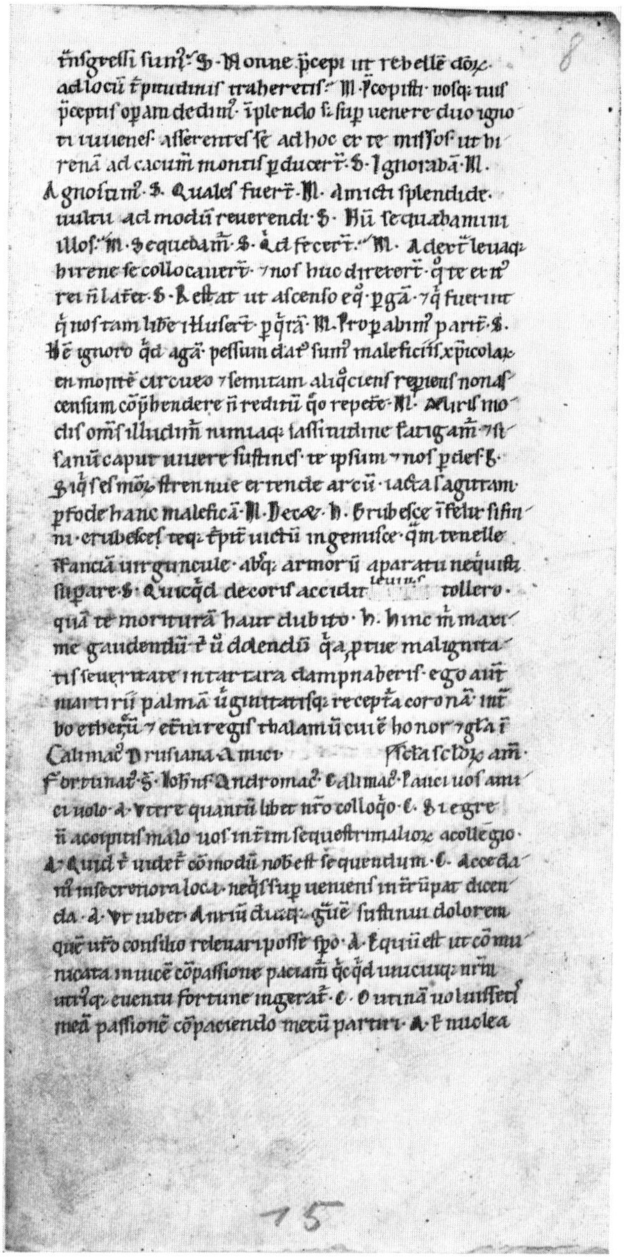

Plate 3. Cologne, Historisches Archiv W 101 ǐ, fol. 8 recto. End of *Dulcitius* and beginning of *Calimachus*. Last quarter of the twelfth century.

distinction made between *u*, *v*, and *iu*. This script is taller, the letters more acute, the abbreviations more frequent, and the alignment even worse than that of the first hand (*Plate 2*).

The general appearance of the lettering is nervous, light, and irregular, characteristics frequently observed in the writing of nuns, to whom it was first ascribed by Conrad Celtes, discoverer of the manuscript at St. Emmeram. Paul von Winterfeld, who edited the manuscript in 1902, basing his opinion on the paleographer Traube's comments on the similar script of a *Homerus Latinus*, also formerly in Regensburg, agreed that No. 1 might be considered the work of nuns.

The origin of this manuscript in Hroswitha's own convent of Gandersheim is most probable. From there it is thought to have been sent by the distinguished Abbess Gerberga (*d.* 1002), daughter of Duke Henry of Bavaria, to their ancestral monastery of St. Emmeram in Regensburg, where it was preserved until the secularization of the monastery in 1803; then, with the other books of the St. Emmeram library, it was sent to the Bavarian National Library at Munich. In 1494, Celtes, a humanist, scholar, and poet, saw and borrowed the manuscript from St. Emmeram, and in 1501 he published it at Nuremberg; he omitted the *Vision of St. John* and the short poem of four elegiac distichs, neither of which appeared in print until 1857, when Bendixen included them in his *Comoedias sex* (see No. 35).

Paul von Winterfeld published the first critical edition of the manuscript, with bibliography, in 1902 (see No. 43).

2. [*Gallicanus, Dulcitius, Calimachus, Abraham*; and other texts]. Cologne, Historisches Archiv W 101ᵻ.

70 ff., vellum, 7½ × 3¹⁵⁄₁₆ inches, 37 lines. Last quarter of XII century.

Written by a proficient scribe using a small, laterally compressed script with vertical ductus and many abbreviations. A date late in the XII century is indicated by the occasional superimposing of the *s* form at the end of a word; *ii* have slanting strokes and *e* is used for the diphthong *æ* (*Plate 3*).

43

The Hroswitha text (ff. 1–16), on the first sixteen leaves of a volume of miscellaneous canonical works, was discovered in Cologne in 1922 by Goswin Frenken (see No. 207). It does not derive from No. 1, and, in some instances, is more complete and the readings are more correct. The absence of introductory matter (prefaces, titles, etc.) is one of the several valid reasons given by Frenken for believing it to have been copied from an early prototype which was sent by Hroswitha to one of the three scholars to whom she appealed for a critical evaluation of her dramas. It is probable that one of these consultants was in the monastery of St. Pantaleon in Cologne, where Frenken thinks the transcript was made. It is regrettable that, among the Cologne manuscripts of this period published by Chroust,* none has a sufficiently similar script to substantiate his theory.

3. [*Maria* and *Sapientia*, fragments]. Klagenfurt, Austria, Studienbibliothek Ms 44.

4 binaries, vellum, 12 × 8½ inches, forming pages 8½ × 6 inches, 24 lines. Late XII or early XIII century.

Written by a capable scribe trained in a well-disciplined scriptorium. The hand is firm and stubby, with very short descenders, the pressure is heavy with little shading and considerable variation in slant. Numerous advanced letter forms rule out an XI-century date and show, instead, that a late XII-or early XIII-century dating is preferable. Among them are the frequent use of round *s* and uncial *d*, the occasional stroking of *i*, the surprising appearance of lozenge-shaped *o*, the bow of *h* with its long down stroke, causing it to resemble *b*, to mention but a few. There are tonic accents, in addition to a full system of punctuation (*Plate 4*).

The Hroswitha texts were discovered in 1925 by Hermann Menhardt (see No. 215), while examining the binding of Klagenfurt 52, a paper manuscript of Robertus Holtgot (i.e., Robert of Holcot, *d.*

*A. Chroust, *Monumenta palaeographica: Denkmäler der Schreibkunst des Mittelalters*, II Series, I Band, Lieferung VII–VIII, Munich, 1911, and II Series, I Band, Lieferung IX, Munich, 1914.

1349), an English divine, *Praelectiones in librum sapientiae*, dated Gaunersdorf, 1417.

The four sheets containing the *Maria* verses (84–275) had been used to line the covers of the volume; they were later removed and assigned the manuscript number Kl. 44. Passages of *Sapientia*, on strips ½ × 12 inches, from the same manuscript (fragments of the play found on ff. 123–126 in No. 1), remain in the binding as the hinges for the Holtgot paper leaves. Menhardt was of the opinion that Kl. 44 (our No. 3) had been copied in the XI century from No. 1, although he himself found so many variants that this theory can hardly be tenable. He traced the provenance of the volume and its binding to the Dominican convent in Vienna, in whose library catalogue of 1513 it is listed as number C 11. He thought that other bindings there might also contain portions of the same Hroswitha manuscript, but Dr. Thomas Kaeppeli, O. P., of the Istituto Storico Domenicano in Rome, has said that he knows of no further fragments of Hroswitha texts in Dominican libraries. Later in the XVI century this manuscript No. 3 belonged to the monastery of St. Paul in Lavanttal whence, in 1786, it came to the Studienbibliothek in Klagenfurt (see No. 226, p. 99).

4. [*Gallicanus* and other texts]. Munich, Bayerische Staatsbibliothek Clm 2552 (formerly Alderspach 22).

182 ff., vellum 12½ × 8¾ inches, 36 lines (432 in all). Early XIII century.

Written by a proficient scribe using many contractions and suspensions. The ductus is firmly vertical, risers and descenders are short, and the ends of the latter terminate with a slight, light curve to the left. The word separation is good, and this with the forked risers and fractura date the script early in the XIII century (*Plate 5*).

The Hroswitha text is written on ff. 1–4 of a volume of 182 leaves, containing lives of saints. It was mentioned, without identification of the author, in a list of the contents of No. 4 by O. Holder-Egger (see No. 161). In 1900 the author was recognized by von Winterfeld, who published his discovery in 1902 (see No. 43), and gave the variants from the text of No. 1 where the play appears on ff. 80–90.

45

The Bayerische Staatsbibliothek obtained this manuscript with the fine library of the Cistercian monastery of the Apostle Peter at Alderspach, Bavaria, at the secularization in 1803.

5. [*Gesta Oddonis*, dramas and poems]. Pommersfelden Castle, Upper Franconia, Library of Count Schoenborn Ms 308 (2883).

137 ff. (misbound), paper, 12×8 inches, 34 lines. Late XV century.

Manuscript texts: f. 1, title page of the transcriber (*Plate 6*); ff. 2–16, Hroswitha, *Gesta Oddonis* (*Plate 7*); ff. 16–16 v, anonymous, *De conversione Saxonum*; ff. 17–101 v, Hroswitha, dramas and poems; and ff. 102–137 v, Aldhelmus, *Carmen de laudibus virginitatis*.

Copied from No. 1 between 1494 and 1501 by Theodore Gresemund, Jr., a citizen of Mainz, without adhering to the order of the original.

Written in two scripts. The first (*Plate 6*) is a rather cramped slanting book minuscule; the second (in which the major part of the manuscript is written) is a handsome, practised bâtarde (*Plate 7*).

The library, now in Pommersfelden Castle, was founded by Lothar Franz (1655–1729), Count of Schoenborn and Archbishop of Mainz, by the wholesale appropriation of the choicest books from the monasteries in his archdiocese (see also No. 43, pp. v and xiv at note 48, and No. 195, Vol. I, p. 632).* His collection, originally housed in his castle at Gaibach, was transferred to Pommersfelden Castle in 1732.

*Bibliotheca Gaibacensis sive Catalogus librorum tam impressorum quam manuscriptorum . . . D. Friderico Carolo episcopo Banbergensi [et Her] bipolensi F. O. duce in ordinem alphabeticum . . . conscriptum. M.D.C. [CXXXII], p. 66, Lit. V., Num. 65 (a manuscript catalogue); Friedrich Karl Gottlob Hirsching, Versuch einer Beschreibung sehenswürdiger Bibliotheken Deutschlands nach alphabetischer Ordnung der Städte, Bd. I, Erlangen, 1786, p. 132, Num. 3 (the Pommersfelden manuscript there assigned to the XIV century); Georg Andreas Göpfert, Katalog, 1830, Num. 2883, typescript catalogue of the library at Pommersfelden [we are indebted to the Rev. Wilhelm Schonath, Librarian of Count Schoenborn, Pommersfelden, for transcripts from the foregoing unprinted catalogues]; Gesellschaft für ältere deutsche Geschichtskunde, Archiv, Vol. 9, Frankfurt, 1847, p. 534; Max Manitius, Geschichte der lateinischen Literatur des Mittelalters, I, Munich, 1911, p. 632.

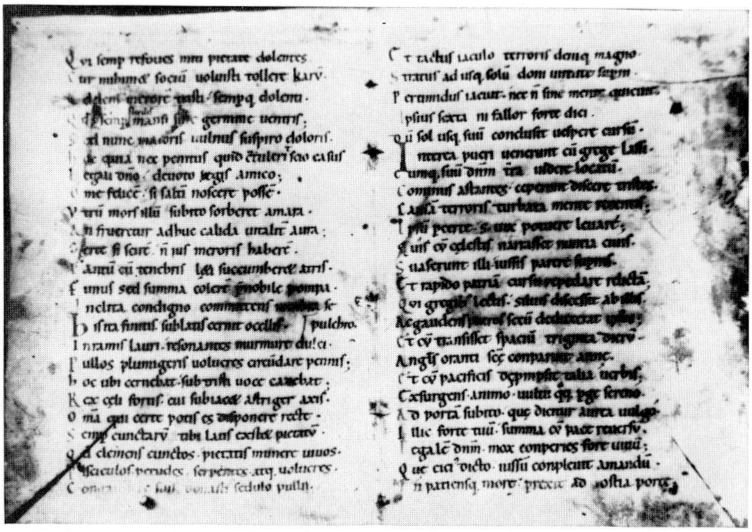

Plate 4. Klagenfurt, Austria Studienbibliothek Ms 44, fol. 1 verso, 4 recto. *Maria*, verses 108–131 and 228–251. Late twelfth or early thirteenth century.

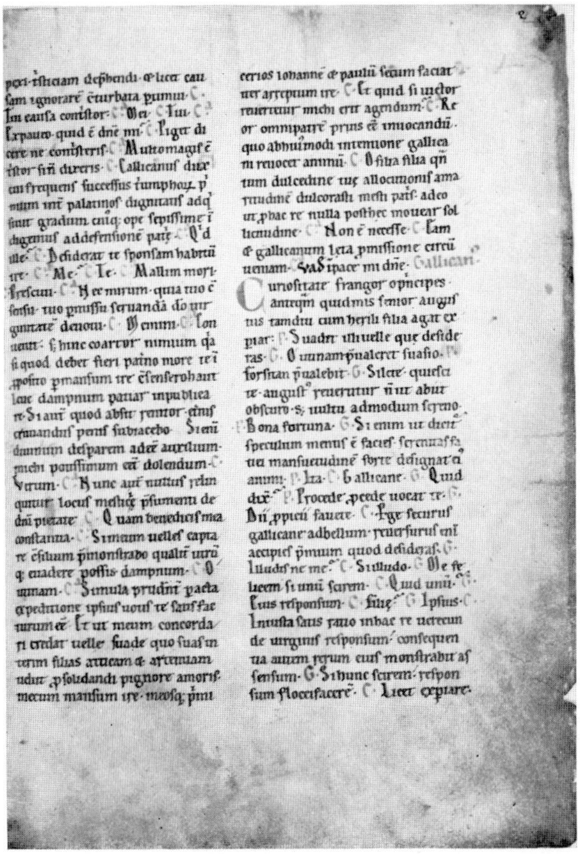

Plate 5. Munich, Bayerische Staatsbibliothek Clm 2552, fol. 2 recto. *Gallicanus*. Early thirteenth century.

Theodorici gresemundi iunioris moguntini
in Rosuidam vestalem Alemannicam Hexastichon
Rosuida phoebeos doctissima tenderet nervos
Rosuida germani gloria magna soli
Sanctorum arguto celebrasti carmine vitas
Collibus modulis nulla fabella tuis
Tu doctum latium superans doctissima nostras
Excellis doctos femina docta viros

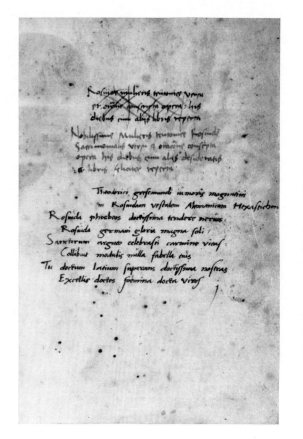

Plate 6. Pommersfelden Castle, Upper Franconia, Library of Count Schoenborn Ms 308 (2883), fol. 1 recto. Title page of the transcriber. Late fifteenth century.

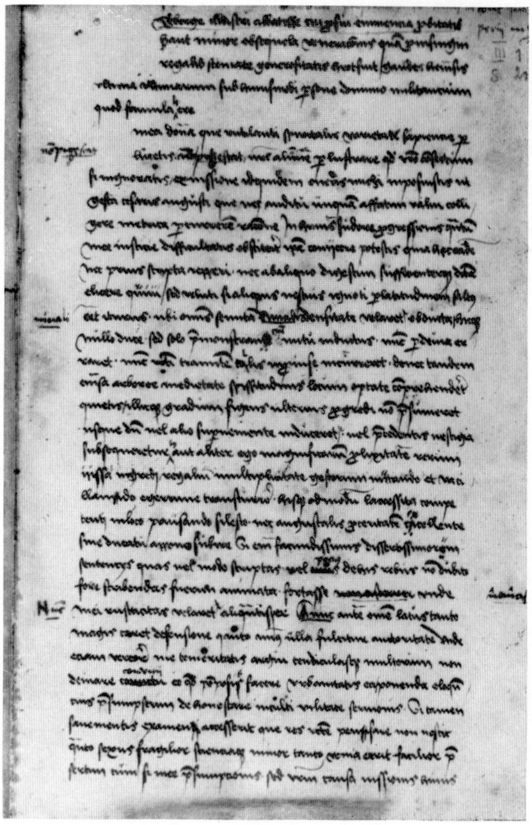

Plate 7. Pommersfelden Castle, Upper Franconia, Library of Count Schoenborn Ms 308 (2883), fol. 2 recto. Beginning of *Gesta Oddonis*. Late fifteenth century.

6. [*Abraham* and other texts]. Heidelberg, Universitätsbibliothek Cod. Pal. Germ. 298.

150 ff., paper, averaging about 12½ × 8¾ inches, 30–34 lines. Early XVI century.

A fair copy, written in a bold, flowing bâtarde script (*Plate 8*).

The translation of *Abraham* into German was made by the poet and scholar, Adam Wernher von Themar (born 1462 in Thuringia), from the 1501 edition of Celtes. It commences with a short introduction by the translator and the dedication of his work to his patron, Philip, Count-Palatine of the Rhine, Duke of Bavaria, to whose sons he was tutor. The colophon (on f. 122) states that the work was completed on the Wednesday after St. Valentine's Day, in 1502 (see Nos. 104 and 183).

Manuscript No. 6 consists of 150 leaves, plus 10 added, according to No. 183, though no mention is made there of 12 misnumbered leaves of the Hroswitha *Abraham*, 101–104, 109, 116–122. The manuscript is made up of three sections. The first and last are a collection of chiefly religious works. The second, a collection of works all translated by Adam Wernher von Themar, including the Hroswitha *Abraham*, appears on ff. 76 and 77–133, and was originally known as Pal. 831.

7. [*Dulcitius*, in Hungarian, and other texts]. Budapest, Egyetemi Könyvtár (University Library) Codex Hungaricus-Universitatis Budapestinensis 6, known as the "Sándor Codex."*

*Concerning the Sándor Codex, see: Zs. Alzeghy *Magyar dramai emlékek a középkortál besseyeiig*, Budapest, 1914; L. Mezey, *Közepkori Magyar irasok*, Budapest, 1957; Friedrich Scharff, *Die deutsche Schrift im Mittelalter*, Frankurt, 1866 (table of alphabets of 1450); Gustav Friedrich, *Uabna knihapalaeografie latinski*, Prague, 1898, p. 176; A. Reinecke, *Die deutsch Buchschrift*, Leipzig 1910, pls. 207, 213; Julius von Farkas, "Die ungarische Literatur Wissenschaft und der deutsche Geist," in *Forschungen und Fortschritte*, Vol. 4, No. 21, July 20, 1928, pp. 215–216.

20 ff., paper, about 7⅛ × 4¹⁄₁₆ inches (182 × 119 mm.), 29–31 lines. Early XVI century.

The manuscript is described as follows by Sándor Szilágyi in No. 153:

"Cod. chart. saec. XVI, 4°, 20.

"a) la–20b, Opusculum hung. in parabolis de coelo et infernis. *Inc.* 'Ezt mongya uala zent pal apastal.' *Expl.* 'mijndönök fordulnak vezzödelmere. In Cristo dilecta domina hunc exemplum excepi de libro fratris Bernardino de Bustij, qui fuit frater Sancti Francisci.'

"Fol. 18ab leguntur: 'notae de tribus illis rebus quae commendantur et reprobantur in persona religiosa, et quas persona religiosa facere debet.'

"Codex 'Sándor-codex' nuncupatus et in Vol. II coll. *Nyelvemléktár* editus (see No. 38)."

The name *Sándor Codex* was given to the manuscript by its discoverer, Ferencz Toldy (1805–1875), in honor of the eminent bibliographer and author of vocabularies, István Sándor.

The translation of *Dulcitius* (ff. 11–16, through line 6) is a free one; the original names of three characters in the drama were changed by the translator; Dulcitius becomes Fabius, Sisinnius is Varius, and Diocletian here appears as a nameless emperor of Turkey. This is the first dramatic play in Hungarian (see No. 239).

The writing shows some of the feminine characteristics previously noted in the early Hroswitha manuscripts. It is a refined, and certainly greatly retarded hand, with poor spacing and alignment, whose appearance, were it not for the information contained in the colophon appearing on leaf 20, would date it somewhere between 1450 and 1475 (*Plate 9*). Some feeble attempts were made to embellish the majuscule letters, with only mediocre effect. L. Katona (see No. 178) thinks the scribe may have been a nun in the Dominican convent on St. Margaret's Island (formerly the Island of Rabbits) in the Danube at Budapest.

Friar Bernardino de Busti, to whom the scribe refers in the past tense, was born in Milan. In 1475 he entered the Franciscan Order in Santa Maria della Misericordia at Melegnano, where he died in 1500. He was noted for his *Rosarium sermonum per totum annum,* and was the author of numerous poems in praise of the Virgin Mary, the first of which was published in 1488–1489 under the title *Corona della beatissima Vergine Maria.**

Very little has been written in English about the *Sándor Codex*; the enlistment of the interest and assistance of János Scholz, the Hungarian scholar, collector, and musician, has permitted the inclusion in this volume of detailed notes on this manuscript for the benefit of English-speaking readers.

János Scholz has made a careful study of the ancient Hungarian texts, based on photographs of the whole of the *Sándor Codex* together with its printed form in No. 38. He supplied the translations needed to identify the beginnings and endings of the various texts, and also gave translations from a number of references containing Hungarian articles on the *Sándor Codex*, as suggested by L. Mattrai, Director of the University Library at Budapest, which were found to be available at the New York Public Library.

Scholz's opinion that the Hungarian *language* of the manuscript was that of a period somewhat earlier than the XVI century (possibly about 1450?) concurs with Meta Harrsen's conclusion that certain aspects of the *handwriting* suggest a date of about 1450–1475 (*Plate 9*). This agrees, in part, with Katona's belief that *Dulcitius* in Hungarian, cited here, is a copy of an *earlier* manuscript translation (see No. 178), although Katona thought that the original translation was probably based on No. 1, which would date it no earlier than about 1494 if one accepts the fact that No. 1 (or any other Hroswitha manuscript) was indeed unknown before Celtes' "discovery" of No. 1 at that time. As to its *latest* possible date, Gyula Zolnai (see No. 170) says: "The date of the manuscript cannot be established from the manuscript itself; György Volf discovered the fact that it is the closing portion of the rather voluminous old codex which, for an unknown reason, was separated during the 1850's, bound in five volumes, and baptized as follows: *Cornides-codex*, part I; *Bod-codex*; *Cornides-codex*, part II; *Booklet about the glory of the holy Apostles*; *Book of Examples* and the *Sándor-codex*. The Bod- and Sándor codices do not disclose their date of origin; however, as the handwriting of the other

*Giuseppe Galli: "Due ignote edizioni della Corona della Vergine," in *Miscellanea bibliografica in memoria di Don Tomaso Accurti*, Rome, 1947, p. 103.

49

portions falls between 1510 and 1521, according to the dates found within, the date of the *Sándor-codex*, after giving it the most careful scrutiny, could not be later than 1530."

Tibor Kardos (see No. 297) considers that the finding of Hroswitha's *Dulcitius* translated into Hungarian in the midst of the devotional and moralizing *Sándor Codex* is a typical example of the new Hungarian humanistic literature of that period. It was natural that it should have been copied out for the Dominican nuns of St. Margaret's Island near Budapest, since, as he says, "this convent had become a real radiating center of Hungarian literature where, from Buda and other regions far away, reading matter of the most extraordinary variety and origin was given to the nuns in translation, besides the significant original material in the native tongue." Also, Kardos is quite convinced that Celtes, in his editing of Hroswitha's plays, indicated that he meant them to be performed: "The action is brief, as generally in any old-Christian play, but varied and dramatically taut; its dialogues are alive and fast." The Hungarian translator, in adapting the names to contemporary events (the recurrent possibility of Turkish invasion, first threatened prior to 1456 and finally accomplished in 1526), evidently carried the same thought in mind: that the play was to be acted. And Kardos conjectures: "Possibly it was performed for the populace at a great city festival, like the Sybilla-play of 1501, by students or members of an artisan's guild play-group."

So much for the tantalizing glimpses of facts, the speculations and uncertainties as to the dates, sources, and background of this little manuscript. The contents, with the identifying words for the beginnings and ends of its various parts, are as follows (given here because there are no titles for any of the separate texts and the whole manuscript runs together in a confusing way).

Leaf 1 begins: *Ezt mongya uala zent pal apastal* . . . (in English, a free translation of the whole of the opening sentence: St. Paul said once to the Corinthians, "It was written that eyes never saw, ears never heard, it never entered the heart of humans what the Lord has prepared for those who love Him . . . ").

Ends at bottom of leaf 10 with a rather interesting alliteration, using musical instruments and musical terms to describe the joy prepared for those who enter heaven and about the horrors awaiting

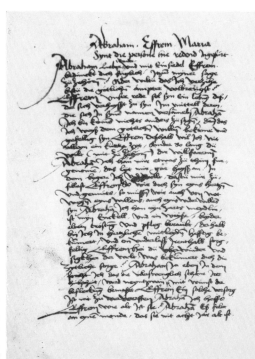

Plate 8. Heidelberg, Universitätsbibliothek Cod. Pal. Germ. 298, fol. 101 verso. Beginning of *Abraham*, in German. Early sixteenth century.

Plate 9. Budapest, Egyetemi Könyvtár (University Library) Codex Hungaricus-Universitatis Budapestinersis 6, fol. 12 verso, 13 recto. *Dulcitius*, in Hungarian. Early sixteenth century.

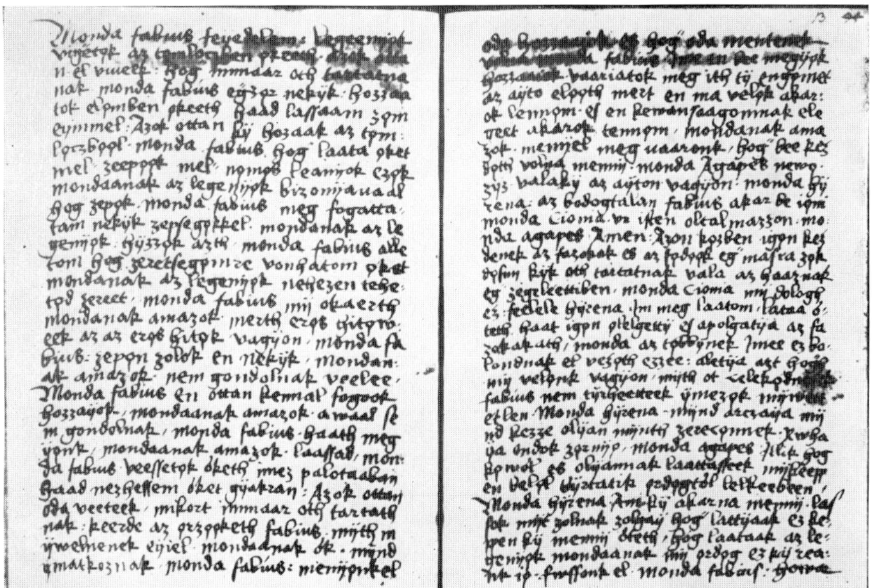

Plate 10. Berlin, Preussische Staatsbibliothek, Theol. lat. fol. 265, fol. 37 verso. End of *Gesta Oddonis* and colophon, column 1; and the *Epistola*, which is usually found preceding the dramas, column 2. First half of the sixteenth century.

those condemned to hell. This appears to be a sort of moralist treatise or admonition to members of a sacred order.

Leaf 11 r, line 1 (*Dulcitius*) begins: *Harom köröztyn leanth ragattak volth el az törökök* . . . (in English: Three Christian maidens have been abducted by the Turks and brought before the Emperor . . .).

[Note: Katona was the first to recognize this as a Hroswitha text; he reported his discovery at a conference of the Budapest Philological Society, May 12, 1899, and it was published (see No. 178).]

Ends on leaf 16 r, line 6: Monda Hijrena: ezön en neköm igön keel örölnom, te neköd igön bankodnod . . . (in English, in full: Said Irene, "While this makes me rejoice, it would cause you despair because on account of your cruelty you have been condemned to hell while I receive the palm of martyrdom and the crown of virginity from Jesus Christ, my betrothed, to whom should go honour and glory throughout eternity.").

Leaf 16 r, line 7 begins: *Im arrol irok zeep tanossaagoth mikeppen kesserty az ördög* . . . (in English, in full: Now I will write a beautiful lesson in what way the devil tempts the virgins, the widows, the married). This text concludes with a short paragraph containing the legend of Abigail.

Ends at leaf 18 r, line 2: . . . *engedye isten hog ig lehessön* (in English: . . . may God permit that it could be thus).

Leaf 18 r, line 3 begins with the Latin referred to in the Szilágyi *Catalogus* (see above).

Ends at line 5 on leaf 18 v, and the rest of that leaf is blank. The text seems to be a kind of conclusion or summary of the matter discussed in the Hungarian text that starts with *"Im arrol* . . . *"*; it was not printed in No. 38 since that work only concerned the Hungarian part of the *Codex*.

Leaf 19 r, line 1 begins: *Baraatoknak kananokoknak apaczaaknak: es egyeb eghaazy embüröknek: kyk čak feyök meg nyreetesseuel es ruhaa viffellessökkel esmertetnek istennek hazwgny* (!) (in English: To friars, canons, nuns and to other people of the church; who, recognized [as such] only because of their shaven heads and garbs . . .). This text deals with the torments of hell prepared for religious people who have not kept their lives unsullied.

Ends on leaf 20 r, line 24: . . . *mynt Im en neköd nyluan meg irtam az töb kenoknak iraassaat mind el haguan mert azokat tudny nem olyan zükseeg* (in English: ... as I have so frankly written you above, it is therefore superfluous to relate all other pains [punishment], because it is not necessary to know about them).

Leaf 20 r, between lines 24 and 25, there is a faint line in the manuscript (and in No. 38 there is an extra space).

Leaf 20 r, line 25 begins: *Apaczaaknak klastromokban vala ég appacza ky mind az többyt föliöl mulva vala penitencia tartassal* ... (in English: There was in a convent a nun, who surpassed all the others in doing penance and hard life ...).

Ends on leaf 20 v: In Cristo dilecta domina hunc exemplum excepi de libro fratris Bernardini de Bustij qui fuit frater sancti francisci.

[NOTE: Ferencz Toldy (see above and No. 126) identifies this last text as an example out of Bernardino de Busti, and seems to indicate that the Latin "colophon" (as given above) actually refers only to it, rather than to the whole of the *Sándor Codex*; the separation of texts as printed in No. 38 seems to confirm this impression.]

8. [*Gesta Oddonis* and other texts]. Berlin, Preussische Staatsbibliothek Theol. lat. fol. 265 (formerly Maria Laach monastery, Eastern Eifel, Rhineland); now Tübingen University Library, depot of the former Preussische Staatsbibliothek.

199 ff., vellum, 11 × 7½ inches, 2 columns. First half of XVI century.

Written by Frater Valerius Meyensis in the Benedictine monastery of Maria Laach, where he died in 1556. It is assumed that the copy was made a year or two after the appearance of the first edition in 1501. It is written in a strong, early XVI-century hand upon palimpsest of the XII century. It is a stubby, fractured gothic book minuscule, with a cursive tendency. The pressure is even, with little shading; the number of abbreviations is kept within reasonable bounds. A transitional feature from the XV to the XVI century is a continued stroking of some of the *i*'s (*Plate 10*).

The Hroswitha text, ff. 2–38, column 1, was copied from Celtes' edition, but it does not adhere strictly to his arrangement of the plays, while the Introduction to the plays appears at the very end of the manuscript. *Gesta Oddonis* concludes: *Nobis solamen dantes clementius Amen* (as in the Celtes edition), appearing here in the manuscript on leaf 37, column 1, and is followed by a copy of the first two lines of Celtes' colophon: *Finis operum Hrosuithe clarissime virginis et monialis Germanice gente Saxonica ortae.* The scribe completes column 1 with his own colophon as follows: *Per me fratrem Valerium Meyensem in hanc formam scriptorum pro quo memor sit mei omnipotens deus.* Then leaf 37, column 2, begins: *Epistola eiusdem ad quosdam sapientes . . . Plene sciis et bene moratis . . .* , which is the beginning of the Introduction to the plays as it appears preceding the plays in the Celtes edition on leaf 4 r, line 32. In this manuscript, the Introduction to the plays ends on leaf 38 r, column 1, line 8.

The volume has a total of 199 leaves and contains, in addition to the Hroswitha text, excerpts from the works of numerous Christian poets by various scribes of the XVI century (see also No. 186).*

*Gesellschaft für ältere deutsche Geschichtskunde, Archiv, Vol. 8, Frankfurt, 1843, p. 839.

Lost Manuscripts

META HARRSEN

9. [Works of Hroswitha]. Altzelle, Cistercian Monastery (near Meissen) Ms 03.

The entry "Opera Hrosvite illustris monialis" appeared in a manuscript entitled *Monasterii Veteris Cellae abbates* dated 1514, which was preserved in the University Library of Leipzig. It was given number 678 by Councillor Ebert, the University Librarian, who compiled the catalogue. When G. H. Pertz visited the Leipzig Library in 1831, he made a note of the entry but did not see the manuscript.*

10. [*Primordia*; and the unique *Vitae paparum SS. Anastasii et Innocentii*]. Gandersheim Abbey.

This manuscript was lent in 1531 to Heinrich Bodo (1470–1553), a monk of the nearby Kloster Klus, who was writing a history of Gandersheim and Klus, a foundation of the former. Bodo refers to the Hroswitha manuscript as one that had been gathering dust for more than six centuries. He is the only person who attests to the existence of Hroswitha's biographies of Gandersheim's two patron saints, written in hexameters. The borrowed manuscript was not returned to Gandersheim, nor, if Bodo transcribed it, did the copy survive. Bodo's work was published by Heinrich Meibom in No. 18.

The autograph manuscript of Bodo's work, in which he mentions Hroswitha several times (e.g., ff. 2, in the *Praefatiuncula*; 39 r; and 41 v and 42 r) is now part of Ms 19.13. Aug. 4° in the Herzog August Bibliothek, Wolfenbüttel.†

Gesellschaft für ältere deutsche Geschichtskunde, Archiv, Vol. 6, Frankfurt, 1831, p. 218, No. 678.

†Dr. Butzmann, Director, Herzog August Bibliothek, Wolfenbüttel, very kindly verified these passages in the manuscript.

11. [*Primordia*]. Hildesheim, Behrens Collection.

Heinrich Böhmer, in his biography of Willigis von Mainz in *Leipziger Studien aus dem Gebiet der Geschichte*, Vol. I, 1895, p. 200, states that there is every foundation for the assumption that Thankmar of Hildesheim, in writing his *Vita Bernwardi* in the XI century (*Monumenta Germaniae Historica, Scriptorum*, Vol. 4), obtained his information concerning the history of Gandersheim from *Primordia*.

Such a manuscript was discovered in 1706 by the physician of Hildesheim, Dr. Conrad Berthel Behrens (*d.* 1736). It was his intention to publish it. However, Johann Georg Leuckfeld (1668–1726) had been granted permission by the Abbess of Gandersheim to write a history of the abbey, and in order to use this text, he persuaded Behrens to sell it to the Abbess. Eighteen verses from *Primordia* had been published previously in No. 19; they are verses 6–23 which relate to Liudolf, the grandfather of Henry I, and are introduced by Nicolaus Schaten with the remark: "Quapropter ab ipsa Roswida hac candido carminis elogio celebratur," but he does not say where he obtained the lines he used.*

To Leuckfeld, therefore, fell the honor of first publishing the complete *Primordia*, which he did in No. 21. Gottfried Wilhelm von Leibniz (1646–1716) used the same manuscript in No. 22, after which it disappeared.

12. [*Primordia*, fragments]. Nordkirchen Castle, District of Ludinghausen, Westphalia, Library of Count Plettenberg.

Some portions of *Primordia* were present in 1725 in an XVIII-century *Catalogus abbatissarum Gandershemensium*, compiled by J. Rosenthal (see also No. 185).†

*This quotation from Schaten's work was supplied by Professor Dr. Klemens Honselmann, Direktor, Erzbischöfliche Akademische Bibliothek, Paderborn.

†Dr. Tross, "Handschriften auf der gräfl. Plettenbergschen Bibliothek zu Nord-kirchen," in *Gesellschaft für ältere deutsche Geschichtskunde, Archiv*, Vol. 6, Frankfurt, 1831, p. 37, No. 13.

13. [Primordia]. Coburg, Library of the former Ducal Castle.

A transcript of the poem was seen there in 1841 by Georg Waitz, who refers to it as "admittedly a new copy." He found it to be independent of previously known transcripts and having some variants from the text printed in *Monumenta Germaniae Historica, Scriptorum* (see No. 11). That publication, edited by G. H. Pertz, had been made f om No. 1 and from a manuscript in the Royal Library at Hanover.*

14. [Primordia]. Hanover, former Royal Library, Case No. VI (Bibl. Meibom No. 64).

This was a XVI-century manuscript on paper, last seen in 1843 by Georg Waitz.†

The compiler of the foregoing list of Hroswitha manuscripts takes pleasure in acknowledging her debt in its preparation to Dr. Zoltán Haraszti, author of "The Works of Hroswitha," in *More Books, Bulletin of the Boston Public Library*, March and April, 1945 (see No. 277), and, in addition to those named in footnotes, to the following correspondents: Dr. G. I. Lieftinck, Rijksuniversiteit, Leiden; Rev. Dr. William Bonniwell, O.P., New York City; Dr. Franz Unter-kircher, Director, Österreichische National Bibliothek, Vienna; Dr. Kuttnig, Bundesstaatliche Studienbibliothek, Klagenfurt; Dr. Joseph Beckmann, Director, Universitätsbibliothek, Freiburg im Breisgau; Dr. H. I. A. Gichtel, Bibliotheksrat, Bayerische Staatsbibliothek, Munich; Dr. Johanna Autenrieth, assistant in the preparation of the *Monumenta Germaniae*, Munich; Dr. J. Weitzmann-Fiedler, Princeton; and Dr. W. Hörmann, Director, Department of Manuscripts, Bayerische Staatsbibliothek, Munich.

---

*Gesellschaft für ältere deutsche Geschichtskunde, Archiv, Vol. 8, Frankfurt, 1843, p. 266.

†*Op. cit.*, p. 637.

Printed Editions
Including Translations

MARJORIE DANA BARLOW

15. Opera, edited by Conrad Celtes. Nuremberg, 1501. Folio.

First printed edition of Hroswitha's works, based on No. 1. Celtes could not include *Primordia* since it was not in the above-cited Munich manuscript; for unknown reasons he excluded Hroswitha's short poem on the *Vision of St. John* which did appear in No. 1, following the dramas.

Illustrations: Eight woodcuts (one a repeat), the first two by Albrecht Dürer (Celtes kneeling and offering the book to Duke Frederick III, three men standing in the background; and Hroswitha kneeling and offering the book to Otto the Great, a nun [Abbess Gerberga?] at center background); and one illustration each for the six plays: *Gallicanus, Dulcitius, Calimachus, Abraham, Pafnutius* (repeated from *Abraham*), and *Sapientia*. These last five woodcuts are usually atributed to Wolf Traut.

There is a reproduction of Dürer's first sketch for the illustration of Hroswitha kneeling before Otto the Great in Friedrich Winkler's *Die Zeichnungen Albrecht Dürers* (4 vols., Berlin, 1936–1939), Plate 249, with a description of the drawing at page 173; Winkler dates it at about 1500. For Dr. Karl Giehlow's first identification of this sketch, see Campbell Dodgson, *Catalogue of Early German and French Woodcuts . . . in the British Museum* (2 vols., London, 1903), Vol. I, pp. 261–262.

Haraszti, Zoltán, "The Works of Hroswitha," in *More Books, Bulletin of the Boston Public Library*, March and April, 1945, pp. 87–119 and 139–173. See also No. 8.

16. Gesta Oddonis, edited by Justus Reuber. *Veterum Scriptorum, qui Caesarum et imperatorum Germanicorum res per aliquot secula gestas literis mandarunt, Tomus unus* . . . (Frankfurt, 1584), pp. 161–180. Folio.

A reprint of *Gesta Oddonis* from the Celtes edition, with a few corrections; Reuber was the first to note the two gaps in the poem. *Veterum scriptorum* was reprinted in Hanover in 1619.

Zeydel, Edwin H., "A chronological Hrotsvitha bibliography through 1700, with annotations," in *The Journal of English and Germanic Philology*, July, 1947, pp. 290–294 (III–19). Zeydel divides his bibliography into four sections, identified as "Part I: Works"; "Part II: Manuscripts"; "Part III: Literature on Hrotsvitha, 1494–1600"; and "Part IV: Literature on Hrotsvitha, 1601–1700." The Reuber edition of the *Gesta Oddonis* is the 19th item listed in Part III; later reference to Zeydel's bibliography in this book will employ a similar method of identifying his citations. See also No. 23.

17. Gesta Oddonis, in *Widukind Korvei* (X century), edited by Heinrich Meibom (1544–1625). *Primi et antiquissimi Saxonicae scriptoris Witichindi* . . . *annalium libri tres* (Frankfurt, 1621), pp. 79–107. Folio.

Widukind was a Saxon monk and historian. To this edition of his works, Meibom added a life of Hroswitha (pp. 80–82), *Gesta Oddonis* (pp. 83–103), and explanatory notes (pp. 103–107).

Zeydel, *op. cit.*, IV–5. See also No. 18.

18. Gesta Oddonis, edited by Heinrich Meibom (or Maybaum) (1638–1700), in *Rerum Germanicarum Tomi III.* Helmstedt, 1688. Folio. Includes life of Hroswitha and notes by Heinrich Meibom (1544–1625) in Tom. I, pp. 705–731.

Illustrations: Engraved portrait bust of Hroswitha facing half left, coat of arms top right, inscribed (above portrait): "T. I, p. 706"; (below portrait): "Helena a Rossow, vulgo Hroswida. Sanctimonialis in Gandersheim." This portrait is quarter-page, three other figures appearing on the same page; it is inserted facing page 44 in Tom. III. For another copy of the portrait see No. 20.

Heinrich Meibom (1638–1700), a German physician and historian, edited this whole volume, but used his grandfather's version of *Gesta Oddonis* as it appeared in No. 17.

Heinrich Bodo's *Syntagma de constructione coenobii Gandesiani* appears in Tom. II, pp. 477–510, covering the history of Gandersheim to the middle of the XIII century. There are certain variations in this important text, as noted below.

Syntagma, now at the Herzog August Bibliothek at Wolfenbüttel (see No. 10), is described by Otto von Heinemann (see No. 177) as in the "autograph der Verfassers," with contents as follows: ff. 1–71, Bodo's *Syntagma*, with events to 1531; ff. 71 v, continuation by another hand until 1589; ff. 94 v, a note by Dr. Marc Holthusen, Dean of Mons Sancti Mauritii, on some legal terms concerning land tenure; and ff. 95–260, Bodo's *Chronicon Coenobii Clusini*.

There are two quite different printed versions of Bodo's *Syntagma*, one in No. 18, and the other in No. 22. Leibniz's version, the latter, is based on Wolfenbüttel Ms 19.13. Aug. 4°.

Note the following key points in the Wolfenbüttel manuscript:

Leaf 2 r, *Praefatiuncula* begins: *Cum optimi cuiusque viri sensus* . . .

[About *Primordia*:] *. . . opusculum illud illustrissimae sanctimonialis feminae Hrosuithae in quo ecclesiae memoratae fundationem heroico canit poemate, fateor, me et accendit, et ad rem propemodum compulit. Hoc namque post sexcentos annos latenter in aliquorum notitiam deductum.* . . . (This little work of the illustrious nun Hroswitha, in which she sings in heroic verse of the foundation of the church, I admit excited me and, so to speak, drove me to the subject. For after six hundred years it came mysteriously to the knowledge of some people . . . [the translation is that of Haraszti (see No. 277)].)

Leaf 3 r, at bottom (last line of *Praefatiuncula*) reads: *Vale, optime lector.*

Leaf 39 r, (in the paragraph concerning the Abbess Hroswitha [d. 906]), reads . . . *non est illa Hrosuitha poëtis* . . . .

Leaves 41 through 42 (concerning Hroswitha's works): *Sub il-lustrissima Domina Garburgi ista secunda vitam egit ac floruit nobilis virgo sanctimonialis Hrosuitha in Saxonia nata, miro ingenio et doctrina clarens, et in utroque scribendi genere admirabiliis, cuius opera sunt ista: Ad virgines sacratas castitatem . . . hortando sermone latino conscripsit.*

[A careful listing of the eight legends by title, and with their opening words.]

De Gestis Ottonum . . . , [with its opening words].

De fundatione coenobii Gandesiani . . . versu hexametro cui praemissit vitas pontificum Anastasii et Innocentii . . . , [with the opening words of *Primordia*:] *Ecce meae supplex humilis devoto mentis.*

[A listing of the six plays, with bracket, and identifying words lined off as follows, at left:]
Comoedias/sex in emu-/lationem theren/tij.

[The final paragraph here reads:] *Graecae etiam linguae notitiam habuit. Rara avis in Saxonia visa est, coetanea Joannis anglici fuit quae doctrina sua papatum meruit.*

Syntagma in Meibom (see No. 18). Bodo's *Syntagma* here is based on a manuscript found in Hanover [Hanover Royal Public Library, Ms XXIII: 548], according to Dr. Butzmann, Director of the Herzog August Bibliothek in Wolfenbüttel. It carries the history of Gandersheim only through the election of Bertha II (about the middle of the XIII century), and ends with the words: *Reliqua desunt in MSto.* It also differs in a number of minor aspects from the Wolfenbüttel manuscript 19.13. Aug. 4°, and from No. 22. The differences between this text and the manuscript, which are pertinent to our check list, are:

Page 479: *Proëmium* (called *Praefatiuncula* in the Ms) begins, as in the manuscript: *Cum optimi cujusque viri sensus . . . .* [About *Primordia*:] *. . . opusculum illud illustrissimae foeminae Hrosuithae, in quo ecclesiae memoratae fundationem heroico canit carmine, fateor me plurimum juvit. Hoc namque post sexcentos annos (nescio quo sydere nobis favente) pulveris ex sinu levatum . . . .* ([I was much assisted by] this little work of the most illustrious woman Hroswitha in which she sings in a heroic poem of the foundation of the church mentioned. For this [work] after six hundred years (I do not know what star favour-

60

ing us) raised out of the dusty hiding place . . . [the translation is that of Dr. Marek Waysblum]).

Page 480 (last line of *Proëmium*) reads: *Vale lector mi candide. 1531.*

Pages 480–482: Bodo's introduction begins: *Scripturo mihi de matre nostrâ ecclesiâ Gandesianâ* . . . (see No. 22, Vol. 3).

Page 491: the paragraph concerning the Abbess Hroswitha contains no clarifying mention of Hroswitha the poet.

Page 493 (concerning Hroswitha's works), the first paragraph reads as given in the manuscript except: . . .*flourit illustris virgo* . . . (instead of *nobilis virgo*); and the list of works is given thus:

Ad virgines sacras castitatem . . . hortando latino sermone.

[A careful listing of the eight legends, with their opening words.]

De Gestis Ottonum . . . , [with its opening words.]

Et praescripta quidem in lucem per calcographos edita habentur cum comoediis sequentibus.

[A listing of the six plays, with bracket and the word *Comoedia* at left of the list, and *In aemulationem/Terentii* at right.]

[The final paragraph reads: *Verum de fundatione coenobii Gandesiani versu hexametro scriptum opus, cui etiam beatissimorum Pontificum Anastasii & Innocentii vitas eodem genere metrorum contextas praemisit, pulveribus longissimis temporibus abditum nostro aevo vix lucem vidit, aliquibus etiam foliis privatum: taceo quod & vetustate nonnulis in locis, non litterae tantum verum & totae sententiae absumtae sunt. Graecae etiam linguae notitiam habuit, coaetanea Joannis Anglici quae doctrinâ suâ Papatum meruit.*

Syntagma in Leibniz (see No. 22). Bodo's *Syntagma* here (covering the history of Gandersheim to 1531 with later additions to 1589 "in another hand") is based on Ms 19.13. Aug. 4°, now in the Herzog August Bibliothek in Wolfenbüttel; except for *Praefatiuncula*, it is different from the version presented in No. 18, for the latter's edition of *Syntagma*, based on another manuscript, had stopped at about the middle of the XIII century. Leibniz, working from the more complete Wolfenbüttel manuscript, wished at first only to fill out in his edition what No. 18 had omitted and to bring the history of the monastery down to as late a date as possible. He presents this material as follows:

61

Vol. 2, p. 330 (directly following the end of Hroswitha's *Primordia*), there is a heading: *Heinrici Bodonis chronici Gandeshemensis supplementum ex MSto*.

Pages 330–331: *Distichon Distrophon* (source unknown).

Pages 331–332: *Praefatiuncula* begins: *Cum optimi cuiusque viri sensus* . . . , and is all almost word for word as given in the Wolfenbüttel manuscript.

Last line reads: *Vale, optime lector*.

(This all differs only in minor respects from Meibom's *Proëmium*). [NOTE: the following three entries were parts of Bodo's work on Gandersheim and Clus, and were taken by Leibniz out of the Wolfenbüttel manuscript:]

Pages 332–335: *Nomina Episcopum Hildesianorum et ordo eorundem* (up to the election of Otto III; with later supplements, "in two different hands," continuing the catalogue).

Pages 335–337: *Nomina Abbatissarum Ecclesiae Gandesianae in ordinem, quo praefuerunt, redacta* (from Hathmodo, the first Abbess, to the election of Gertrudis in 1504); this is followed by a continuation of the catalogue to 1589 "in another hand," and the note by Holthusen on various legal terms relative to land tenure.

Pages 337–345: *Syntagma* from the XIII century to 1531.

When it came to publishing Vol. 3 of *Scriptores*, Leibniz decided that Meibom's version ought to be given in full, with Leibniz's own corrections and emendations from the Wolfenbüttel manuscript. He presents that material as follows:

Vol. 3, p. 701, is headed: *Fr. Henrici Bodonis Syntagma de Ecclesia Gandesiana ex MSto emendatum atque supplementum*. This text covers the history of Gandersheim to the middle of the XIII century; it begins (without *Praefatiuncula* or *Proëmium*):

Page 701: *Scripturo mihi de matre nostra ecclesia Gandesiana* . . . ; and what follows agrees fairly closely with Meibom, except for the various emendations by Leibniz from the Wolfenbüttel manuscript, e.g., p. 710 (in the paragraph concerning the Abbess Hroswitha): an insert in parentheses (in Leibniz's own words) warns that the Abbess is not be be confused with Hroswitha the poet.

Page 712 (concerning Hroswitha's works) reads: . . . *floruit illustris virgo* . . . (this follows Meibom; the Ms reads *nobilis virgo*).

And the listing of works follows Meibom except that, in the description of *Primordia* and the lives of the Popes in the last paragraph, Leibniz inserts in square brackets the following words from the Ms: [*Rara avis in Saxonia visa est.*], between ... *notitiam habuit.*, and *Coaetanea* ... ; and, [*Incipit: Ecce meae supplex humilis devoto mentis.*] (the opening words of *Primordia*), between ... *absumtae sunt.*, and *Graecae etiam.* ...

Page 727 (end of text) reads: *Quae hic desunt in editione Meibomiana, exhibentur ex MSC Gvelfebytano Tome II, page 339, Script. Brunsvicensia illustrantium.*

19. "Primordia" (fragments) in Nicolaus Schaten (1608–?), *Annalium Paderbonnensium II Partes*, Münster, 1693. Folio.

Primordia, lines 6–19 and 21–23, on p. 128 of Part I. This is the first appearance in print of any part of *Primordia*, the text differing slightly from other published forms, and the source unknown. A new edition of *Annalium*, with a third part added by J. E. Strunk, appeared in Münster in 1774–1775.

Zeydel, *op. cit.*, IV–16. See also No. 10.

20. Opera [*Collected Works*], edited by H. L. Schurtzfleisch. Wittenberg, 1707. Quarto.

A re-editing of No. 15, with the life of Hroswitha by Heinrich Meibom (1544–1625) and his notes on *Gesta Oddonis* (see No. 17).

Illustration. Woodcut portrait bust of Hroswitha, facing half left, with coat of arms at top right. Inscribed at top left "Doctissima haec Virgo Seculo X. Floruit," and below portrait "Hroswitha, Sanctimonialis. In Gandersheim." This appears to be a copy of the engraved portrait in No. 18.

21. "Primordia," in Johann Georg Leuckfeld (1688–1726), *Antiquitates Gandersheimenses*, Wolfenbüttel, 1709, pp. 409–426.

This is the first printing of the whole of *Primordia*, only a fragment

63

of which had been published in No. 19. For Leuckfeld's manuscript source, see No. 11. The text was reprinted in Leuckfeld's *Antiquitates monasticae*, published in Wolfenbüttel, 1710–1723. There is also an article on Hroswitha and her works, pp. 271–276. Leuckfeld was a German numismatist and historian.

Illustrations. Fourteen engraved plates: five views of Gandersheim, Brunshausen, and Clus and nine portraits, including one of Hroswitha (portrait bust, facing half right, coat of arms at top left, apparently a reversed form of that found in No. 20); it is inscribed at bottom "Helena a Rossow, vulgo Hroswida Sanctimonialis in Gandersheim."

Haraszti, *op. cit.*, pp. 98 and 114.

22. "Primordia," in Gottfried Wilhelm von Leibniz (1646–1716), ed., *Scriptores rerum Brunsvicensium illustrationi inservientes*, 3 vols. in all: Vol. 1, Hanover, 1707 (containing no Hroswitha material), Vols. 2 and 3, Hanover, 1710, 1711. Folio.

Primordia in Vol. 2, pp. 319–330.

Bodo, H., *Syntagma*, in Vol. 2, pp. 330–345, and Vol. 3, pp. 701–727. See No. 18 for extended notes on certain variations in this important text.

Leibniz was a German mathematician and philosopher.

Zeydel, *op. cit.*, III–13.

23. "Gesta Oddonis," in Justus Reuber, ed. *Veterum scriptorum . . . tomus unus, a Iusto Reubero olim editus, nova hac editione . . . curante Georgio Christiano Ioannis*, revised edition, Frankfurt, 1726, pp. [221]–250. Folio.

Gesta Oddonis given here includes the notes made by Meibom, cited in Nos. 17 and 18.

Zeydel, *op. cit.*, III–19. See also No. 16.

CAPUT XXX.

HROSWITHÆ
CANONISSÆ GANDERSHEIMENSIS,

DE
CONSTRUCTIONE
COENOBII GANDERS-
HEIMENSIS,
CARMEN

hactenus desideratum
& nunc
primùm editum

à
J. G. Leuckfeld.

Fff   Pro-

Title page of Hroswitha's *Carmen de primordiis et fundatoribus coenobii Gandersheimensis* [*Primordia*], from Johann Georg Leuckfeld's *Antiquitates Gandersheimenses*, Wolfen-büttel, 1709. The first printing of the complete *Primordia* appeared in this book.

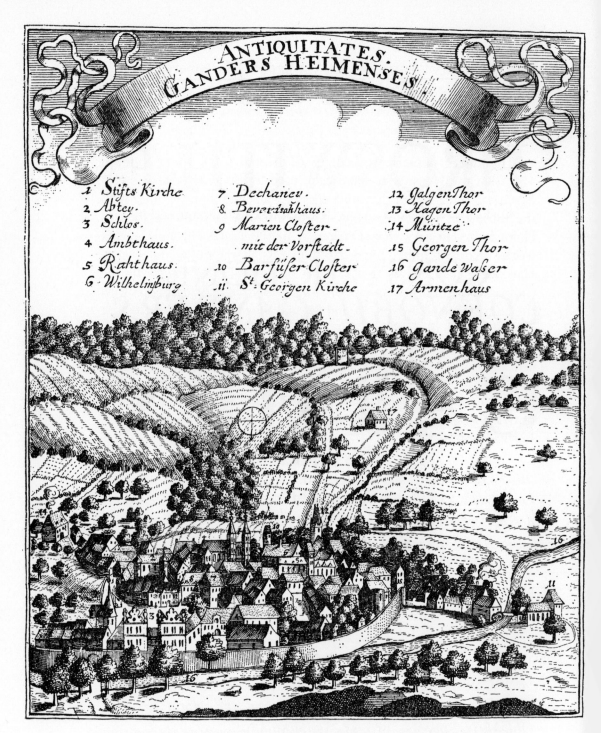

Map of old Gandersheim. Engraved plate from Johann Georg Leuckfeld, *Antiquitates Gandersheimenses*, Wolfenbüttel, 1709.

24. "Primordia" in Johann Christoph Harenberg (1696–1774), *Historia ecclesiae Gandershemensis . . . in supplementum . . . scriptorum rerum Brunsvicensium Leibnizianae adornatum,* Hanover, 1734, pp. 469–476. Folio.

Harenberg, a German theologian, maintains (p. 3 and Note, p. 472) that the Hroswitha manuscript used by Bodo as a basis for his *Syntagma* remained in the monastery of Clus, and that, together with the library of this monastery, it got into the Bibliotheca Julia of Helmstedt. He says that *Primordia*, in the Leuckfeld and Leibniz works (Nos. 21 and 22) was based on a manuscript of a later origin. Harenberg also claims that, for his own version of *Primordia*, he compared the first manuscript of *Primordia* (that used by Bodo) with the later one used in Nos. 21 and 22, and thus here compiled the first critical edition of the work.

Historia includes an interesting bibliography of XVI- and XVII-century works relative to Hroswitha.

Köpke, Ernst Rudolf Anastasius, *Hrotsuit von Gandersheim* (Vol. II of *Ottonische Studien zur deutschen Geschichte im zehnten Jahrhundert*), Berlin, 1869, p. 20.

25. "Gallicanus," translated into German by Johann Christoph Gottsched (1700–1766), in *Nöthiger Vorrath zur Geschichte der deutschen dramatischen Dichtkunst,* 2 vols., Leipzig, 1757; 1765. Octavo.

A discussion of Hroswitha's plays, Vol. 1, pp. 4–10, and Vol. 2, pp. 6–39. This is the first publication of any of Hroswitha's plays in translation; for XVI-century manuscript translations see Nos. 6 and 7.

Haraszti, *op. cit.*, p. 101. See also No. 282, p. 27.

26. "Calimachus" and "Dulcitius," in [William Hayley] (1745–1820), *A Philosophical, Historical and Moral Essay on Old Maids,* 3 vols., 3rd ed., London, 1793.

Calimachus and *Dulcitius* (both in Latin) in the Appendix to Vol. 3; these are preceded by Hroswitha's Preface to the plays (translated into English). Vol. 3 also contains an article on Hroswitha on pp. 51 ff.

Illustrations. Engraved plate copied from a woodcut in No. 15: Hroswitha kneeling and offering the book to Otto the Great; the other illustrations have nothing to do with Hroswitha.

See also No. 102.

27. "Abraham," "Calimachus," and "Dulcitius," translated into French and edited by C. Magnin, in *Théâtre Européen: Théâtre antérieur à la Renaissance*, Paris, Imprimerie de E. Duverger, Guérin et Cie., 1835, pp. 1–30.

28. "Pafnutius," translated into French by and with an introduction by C. Magnin, "Hrosvita, de la comédie au dixième siècle: Paphnuce et Thaïs," in *Revue des deux mondes*, Series IV, Vol. 20, Paris, 1839, pp. 441–480.

29. "Primordia" and "Gesta Oddonis," in *Monumenta Germaniae Historica*, edited by G. H. Pertz, *Scriptorum*, Vol. 4, Hanover, 1841, pp. 302–335.

Primordia is here based on a manuscript found in the Royal Library at Hanover; *Gesta Oddonis* is based on No. 1 (see Nos. 13 and 14).

Haraszti, *op. cit.*, pp. 101–102.

30. *Théâtre de Hrotsvitha* [Collected plays], in French, translated and edited by Charles Magnin. Paris, 1845.

The Latin text of No. 1, with the French translation opposite.

Illustration. Reproduction of one woodcut from No. 15: Hroswitha kneeling and presenting the book to Otto the Great.

Haraszti, *op. cit.*, p. 101. See also No. 282, pp. 38–39.

31. Das älteste Drama in Deutschland: Die Comödien der Nonne Hrotswitha von Gandersheim [Collected plays], in German verse, translated by J. Bendixen. 2 vols. Altona, 1850; 1853.

The six plays in German Knittelvers.

See No. 282, p. 39.

32. "Gesta Oddonis," translated into German by K. F. A. Nobbe, in *Geschichte Oddos des Grossen* (Programme, Nikolaischule, Leipzig), Leipzig, 1851, pamphlet.

A second edition was published in 1852.

33. "Opera," in *Patrologiae cursus completus, Tomus CXXXVII,* Series Latina, *Tomus I,* edited by J.-P. Migne, Paris, 1853, columns 939–1208.

Includes the notes of both Heinrich Meiboms and those of Schurtzfleisch and Celtes. *Opera* is based on No. 20, *Primordia* on No. 29.

Columns 1169–1208 contain an "Appendix ad opera Hrotsuithae: Vita et obitu Hathumodae," and an "Index Latinatis in Hrotsuithae opera." The book was reprinted in 1879 with the Hroswitha material appearing in columns 939–1210.

34. Poésies Latines [Selected poems], in French. Latin text with free French translation by Vignon Rétif de la Bretonne. Paris, 1854.

These poems do not include *Primordia* or *Gesta Oddonis*.

35. Comoedias sex [Collected plays], edited by J. Bendixen. Lübeck, 1857.

Based on No. 1, and includes the first printing of Hroswitha's *Vision of St. John,* a poem of 35 lines found in the manuscript following the dramas, but ignored by Celtes and all other editors prior to Bendixen. The book was reprinted in 1862.

See No. 277, pp. 373–376.

36. Werke [Collected works], edited by K. A. Barack. Nuremberg, 1858.

A critical edition based chiefly on No. 1, but including the *Vision of St. John* and the four elegiac distichs; Barack completed *Werke* by adding *Primordia* from another source.

Haraszti, *op. cit.*, p. 102.

37. "Primordia" and "Gesta Oddonis," translated into German by T. G. M. Pfund, in *Der Hrotsuitha Gedicht über Gandersheims Gründung und die Thaten Kaiser Oddo I* (Series title: *Die Geschichtsschreiber der deutschen Vorzeit, X Jahrhundert*, Vol. 5). Berlin, 1860.

38. "Dulcitius," in Hungarian in *Nyelvemléktár regi Magyar codexek és nyomtatvanyok* (*Collection of Linguistic Relics of Ancient Hungarian Mss and Printed Books*), Vol. 2, Budapest, 1874, pp. 227–232.

This is the first printing of *Codex Hungaricus Universitatis Budapestinensis 6* (*Sándor Codex*), of which *Dulcitius* (without title) forms a part; the translator is unknown (see No. 7). The whole of the *Sándor Codex* occupies pp. 215–238 in *Nyelvemléktár*, which is available at the Library of Congress in Washington, D. C.

39. "Primordia" and "Gesta Oddonis," translated into German by T. G. M. Pfund and edited by W. Wattenbach, in *Der Hrotsuitha Gedicht über Gandersheims Gründung und die Thaten Kaiser Oddo I* (Series title: *Die Geschichtsschreiber der deutschen Vorzeit, X Jahrhundert*, Vol. 5). Leipzig, 1888.

These translations are based on the Latin edition by G. H. Pertz, cited in No. 29. The second edition was published in Leipzig in 1891 and it was printed again in 1941.

40. *Die Dramen* [collected plays], in German, translated by O. Piltz. Leipzig, [c. 1889].

There was another edition of this work with the date 1889 on the title page, and a later edition published [c. 1895].

See also Nos. 56 and 72.

41. "Gesta Oddonis," "Gongolfus," and "Abraham" in German in Wilhelm Gundlach, *Hrotsvitha's Ottolied* (Series title: *Heldenlieder der deutschen Kaiserzeit . . . Erster Band*), Innsbruck, 1894.

A critical study of Hroswitha's work, including a translation of *Gongolfus* (pp. 241–256), *Abraham* (pp. 271–374), and *Gesta Oddonis* (pp. 345–404).

42. *Pafnutius*, translated into French by A.-Ferdinand Herold. Paris, 1895.

The Hroswitha Club copy is one of 249 copies printed; it is in pamphlet form.

Illustrations. There are illustrations throughout the text by various artists.

43. *Opera* [collected works], edited by Paul von Winterfeld (Series title: *Scriptores rerum Germanicarum in usum scholarum ex monumentis Germaniae historicis*). Berlin, 1902.

The most erudite edition of *Opera*, based on a careful paleographical study of No. 1; includes the *Vision of St. John*.

Haraszti, *op. cit.*, pp. 157–161.

44. *Opera* [collected works], edited by Karl Strecker (Series title: *Bibliotheca Teubneriana*). Leipzig, 1906.

Strecker's edition is based on No. 1.

Haraszti, *op. cit.*, pp. 102, and 163–164. See also No. 65.

45. *Oeuvres dramatiques* [collected plays], in French, with introduction and literal translation by C. Vellini, Paris, 1907.

The text is based on No. 1.

46. *Commedie* [selected plays] (excerpts only), selected by F. Ermini (Series title: Testi romanzi per uso delle scuole). Rome, 1910.

Dulcitius, scenes II–VI; *Calimachus*, scenes I–IV; *Abraham*, scenes V–VII; and *Pafnutius*, scenes II–V. All texts are in Latin.

47. "Dulcitius" and "Abraham," in German verse, in Paul Karl Rudolf von Winterfeld (1872–1905), *Deutsche Dichter des lateinischen Mittelalters in deutschen Versen*, edited by H. Reich, Munich, 1913.

The plays (here using Bendixen's German translation, in No. 31) appear on pp. 362–401; there is an article on Hroswitha on pp. 103–110, and another article, "Hrotsvits literarische Stellung" (reprinted from No. 187), appears on pp. 445–524.

See No. 279, p. 444, Note 7.

48. *Dulcitius*, translated into English by A. F. McCann, Elmira, N. Y., privately printed, 1916. Pamphlet.

This translation was made to serve as an example of the comedies of Hroswitha for classroom demonstration at Cornell University, Ithaca, N. Y. It was based on No. 44.

49. *I poemetti di Hrotsvit* [collected poems], (Latin text), edited and with an introduction by F. Ermini in *Poeti epici Latini del secolo X*, Rome, Istituto Angelo Calogera, 1920, pp. 1–38 (includes a bibliography).

50. *Abraham*, translated into French by J. Cuzin. Paris, 1921.

51. *Calimachus*, translated into German and put into play form in two acts by Else Schulhoff, in *Die Erwachung des Calima-chus: Ein Schauspiel*, Berlin, 1921.

This translation is based on No. 35.

52. *Abraham*, translated into English by R. S. Lambert. Limited to 100 copies. Wembly Hill, Middlesex, The Stanton Press, 1922. Illustrations by Agnes L. Lambert.

53. *Calimachus*, translated into English by R. S. Lambert. Limited to 75 copies. Wembly Hill, Middlesex, The Stanton Press, 1923. Illustrations by Agnes L. Lambert.

54. *The Plays of Roswitha*, collected plays translated into English by H. J. W. Tillyard, London, 1923.

See No. 283, p. 39: "The best English version; a careful and vigorous translation by a Birmingham scholar."

55. *The Plays of Hroswitha*, collected plays translated into English and edited by Christopher St. John, pseud. [Christa-bel Marshall] (Series title: *The Medieval Library*), London, 1923.

See No. 283, p. 39: "A smooth rendering into prose."

56. *Die Dramen* [collected plays], translated into German and with biographical material by O. Piltz, Leipzig, 1925.

See Nos. 40 and 72.

57. *Le Commedie Latine* [collected plays], translated into Italian and with an introduction by S. Dolenz, Rome, 1926 (Series title: *Cultura Medievale*, No. 1).

"Prima traduzione Italiana"; "Elenco bibliographico," pp. xvi–xx.

58. "Theophilus" and "Calimachus," in *Deutsche Dichtungen des lateinischen Mittelalters für den deutsch- und latein Unterricht*, edited by J. Klimberg and J. Schulte (Series title: *Aschendorffs Sammlung lateinischer und griechischer Klassiker*), Münster i/W, 1926, pp. 47 ff.

59. *Hroswitha-Gedenkfeier im Tausendjährigen Gandersheim, 11–13 June, 1926*, Bad Gandersheim, 1926.

60. *Drammi mistici* [collected plays], translated into Italian by T. Sorbelli (Series title: *Mistici*, No. 3), Lanciano, 1927.

61. *Teatro scelto* [collected plays], in Italian, translated by G. Bosio, critical introduction by S. D'Amico. Milan, 1927.

62. *Abraham*, translated into English by W. H. Kent, in *The Tablet*, London, 1928.

63. "Abraham," translated into German and with an introduction by C. Harms, in *Festschrift zur Vierhundertjahrfeier des Alten Gymnasiums zu Bremen*, Bremen, 1928, pp. 208–228.

64. *Abraham*, translated into French as "Chute et conversion de Marie, nièce de l'ermite Abraham," translated and with an introduction in "Le millénaire de Hrotsvitha," by Fritz Norden, in *Revue d'Allemagne*, Paris, 1930, pp. 769–794.

65. *Opera* [collected works], edited by Karl Strecker (Series title: *Bibliotheca Teubneriana*), 2nd ed., Leipzig, 1930.

Based on No. 1, but this edition incorporates the variant readings of the Cologne manuscript for the first time (see No. 2), and includes the *Vision of St. John*, which was part of No. 1 but was omitted by Celtes (see No. 15). It also includes *Primordia*, from various published sources.

Haraszti, *op. cit.*, pp. 102 and 163–164. See also 1st edition, No. 44.

66. Selected works (*Theophilus, Dulcitius, Gesta Oddonis*, and *Primordia Gandeshemensis*), edited by H. Walther, in *Ausgewählte Dichtungen* (Series title: *Lateinische und griechische Lesehefte*, No. 12), Leipzig and Bielefeld, 1931.

Bibliography pp. 111–113.

67. "Calimachus," translated into German by H. Homeyer, in *Die Wiedererweckung der Drusiana und des Calimachus*, Hamburg, 1931.

Latin text at top of each page, with German at bottom.
Illustrations. Two woodcuts reproduced from No. 15: Hroswitha kneeling and presenting her book to Otto the Great, and the illustration for *Calimachus*.

68. "Abraham" and "Gallicanus," translated into English by John Heard, in *Poet Lore*, Vol. 42, No. 4, Spring Issue, Boston, 1935, pp. 299–328.

69. "Dulcitius," translated into English and edited by J. R. Taylor, in *European and Asiatic Plays*, Boston, 1936, pp. 239–250.

70. *Werke* [collected works], in German, translated by Helene Homeyer, Paderborn, 1936.

Includes *Primordia* and the *Vision of St. John* ("an abbreviated paraphrase," according to Zeydel in No. 277).

Illustrations. Five reproductions from No. 15: Hroswitha kneeling and presenting her book to Otto the Great, and the illustrations for *Gallicanus*, *Calimachus*, *Abraham*, and *Sapientia*.

71. Selected works translated into English and with a commentary by Sister M. Gonsalva Wiegand, in *The non-dramatic works of Hroswitha*, St. Louis, Mo., 1936 (thesis, Ph.D., St. Louis University).

Latin text and translation on facing pages. Bibliography on pp. 269–271.

See No. 283, p. 40.

72. Collected plays translated into German by O. Piltz, *Die Dramen*, newly edited by F. Preissl (Series title: *Reclams Universal-Bibliothek*), Leipzig, 1942.

See Nos. 40 and 56.

73. "Gesta Oddonis" and "Primordia" translated into English, and with an introduction by Sister Mary Bernardine Bergman in *Hroswithae liber tertius*, Covington, Ky., 1943 (thesis, Ph.D., St. Louis University, St. Louis, Mo.).

Based on the Latin text of Nos. 44 and 65. Bibliography pp. 161–168. Latin and English texts on facing pages.

74. "Dulcitius," in English, translator's name not given, in *Film and Theatre Today*, edited by Montague Slater and Arnold Rattenbury, London, 1948, pp. 21–24.

75. [Collected plays], translated into Dutch and with an introduction by J. H. E. Endepols, in *Leesdrama's* (Series title: *Monumenta Christiana*, Series 2, part 1), Utrecht and Brussels, 1950.

76. [Collected plays], translated into Italian by C. Cremonesi in *Tutto il teatro* (Series title: *Biblioteca universale Rizzoli*), Milan, 1952.

77. "Dulcitius" and "Abraham," translated into German by Karl Langosch, in *Geistliche Spiele: Lateinische Dramen des Mittelalters mit deutschen Versen*, Basel, 1947, pp. 5–89; "Zur Hrotsvit von Gandersheim," pp. 257–259.

The translations of the plays are based on No. 65. Latin text appears on one side with German translation opposite.

References to Hroswitha

And Her Writing

MARJORIE DANA BARLOW

78. Johannes Tritheim (1462–1516), *De scriptoribus ecclesiasticis*, Basel, 1494. Folio.

First printed record of Hroswitha's works; mentions the six plays, *Gesta Oddonis*, and three of the legends, on leaf 59; the book was reprinted in Cologne in 1546. Tritheim was an important humanist, successively Abbot of Sponheim and of St. Jacob's in Würzburg.

Zeydel, *op. cit.*, III; Stillwell, Margaret B., *Incunabula in American Libraries. A Second Census*, New York, 1940, T410. See also Nos. 79, 88, 89, and 94.

79. Johannes Tritheim, *Catalogus illustrium virorum*, Mainz, 1495. Quarto.

Leaves 9 and 10 contain an elaboration of the notes on Hroswitha given first in No. 78.

Zeydel, *op. cit.*, III–2; Stillwell, *op. cit.*, T392. See also Nos. 88, 89, and 94.

80. Sebastian Brant (1458–1521), *Varia carmina*, Basel, 1498. Quarto.

Contains a ten-line epigram "In laudem Rosuide mulieris poetridos." The author was a German humanist and satiric poet.

Zeydel, *op. cit.*, III–3; Stillwell, *op. cit.*, B977; *Gesamtkatalog der Wiegendrucke*, Vols. 1–7 and Part I of Vol. 8, Leipzig, 1925–1942, 5068. See also Nos. 6, 7, and 14.

81. Heinrich Bebel (c. 1472–1516), *Epistola ad Ioannem Nauclerum alias Fergenhans, qui auctores legendi sint novitiis ad comparandam eloquentiam*, Pforzheim, 1504.

Mentions Hroswitha twice. The author was a German scholar and poet.

Zeydel, *op. cit.*, III–5; Köpke, *op. cit.*, p. 248.

82. Eques Mellerstatinus Chilianus (i.e., Knight of Melrichstadt), *Comedia gloriose parthenices et martiris Dorothee agoniam passionemque depingens*, Leipzig, 1507. Quarto.

Mention of Hroswitha in Foreword.

Zeydel, *op. cit.*, III–6.

83. Battista Fregoso [in Latin: Fulgosius] (c. 1435–1509), *De dictus factisque memorabilibus collectanea*, translated into Latin by Camillo Ghilini, Milan, 1509. Folio.

Praises Hroswitha's learning and fame, leaf [hh 7] recto and verso; based chiefly on No. 78. No record has been found of Fregoso's work having been published prior to 1509, in either Italian or Latin. The author was one of the Doges of Genoa.

Zeydel, *op. cit.*, III–7.

84. Aventinus [in German: Johannes Thurnmaier, Turmair, Thurmayr, or Turmeir] (1477–1534), *Imperatoris Henrici Quarti vita: Epistola ad Ambrosium*, Augsburg, 1518. Quarto.

Celtes' editing of Hroswitha's works mentioned; the book was reprinted in *Samtliche Werke herausgegeben von der Kgl. senschaften*,

6 vols. in 7, Munich, 1881–1908 (Hroswitha mentioned in Vol. 1, p. 604).

Zeydel, *op. cit.*, III–9; Köpke, *op. cit.*, p. 6. See also No. 10.

85. Johannes Cuspinianus [in German: Spiesshaymer] (1473–1529), *De Caesaribus atque imperatoribus Romanis opus insigne*, Strassburg, 1540. Folio.

On p. 376 Cuspinianus, a German physician and historian, speaks of Hroswitha's contemporary poem on Otto as rather crude, but considers it astonishing that it could have been written at all by a Saxon woman of that period.

Zeydel, *op. cit.*, III–10.

86. Lilio Gregorio Giraldi [in Latin: Lilius Gregorius Gyraldus] (1479–1552), *Historiae poetarum . . . dialogi decem, quibus scripta et vitae eorum sic exprimuntur*, Basel, 1545. Octavo.

About Hroswitha, p. 665. The author was an Italian poet and archaeologist.

Zeydel, *op. cit.*, III–12.

87. Conrad von Gesner (1516–1565), *Bibliotheca universalis sive catalogus omnium scriptorum*, Zurich, 1545–1549. Folio.

About Hroswitha, fol. 586.

Zeydel, *op. cit.*, III–11.

88. Johannes Tritheim, *Chronicon insigne monasterii Hirsaugiensis*, Basel, 1559. Folio.

Material on Hroswitha taken from No. 79.

Zeydel, *op. cit.*, III–8. See also Nos. 78, 89, and 94.

89. Johannes Tritheim, *Opera Historica*, . . . Frankfurt, 1601. Folio.

This contains the first published edition of Tritheim's *Annalium Hirsaugiensium Tomi II*, a manuscript begun in 1511 and completed in 1513. The information about Hroswitha repeats that found in No. 79.

Zeydel, *op. cit.*, III–8. See also Nos. 78 and 94.

90. Prudencio de Sandoval (c. 1560–1621), *Antiquedad de la ciudad e eglesia catedral de Tuy*, Braga, 1610. Octavo.

Discussion of Hroswitha's story of Pelagius, p. 62. The author was a Spanish historian, successively Bishop of Tuy and of Pamplona.

Zeydel, *op. cit.*, IV–4.

91. Gerhard Johannes Vossius (1577–1649), *De historicis Latinis libri tres*, Amsterdam, 1627. Quarto.

About Hroswitha, in Book II, pp. 41 and 351. In another edition (or issue?) published in Leiden in 1627, Hroswitha is mentioned on pp. 328–329, according to the Leningrad-Saltykov Library. There was a later edition published in Leiden in 1651. Vossius was a Dutch philologist and historian.

92. [Remi] Casmiro Oudin (1638–1717), *Supplementum de scriptoribus vel de scriptis ecclesiasticis a Bellarmino omissis: Ad annum 1460*, Paris, 1686. Octavo.

About Hroswitha, pp. 311–312.

93. William Cave (1637–1713), *Scriptorum ecclesiasticorum historia literaria a Christo nato usque ad saeculum XIV; XV*, 2 vols. London, 1688; 1698. Folio.

About Hroswitha, in Vol. 2, p. 108. The book was reprinted in

1720, 1740–1743, and again 1741–1745. The author was an English ecclesiastical historian and patristic scholar.

Zeydel, *op. cit.*, IV–14.

94. Johannes Tritheim, *Annalium Hirsaugiensium*, edited by J. Mabillon, Saint Gallen, 1690. Folio.

This is the best edition of *Annalium*, which was first published in 1601 (see No. 89). It contains material on Hroswitha that first appeared in No. 79.

Zeydel, *op. cit.*, III–8. See also Nos. 78 and 88.

95. Franz Christian Paullini (1643–1711), *Das hoch- und wohlgelehrte deutsche Frauenzimmer*, Frankfurt, 1705. Octavo.

Hroswitha mentioned, p. 127. The author was a German physician and naturalist. The book was reprinted in 1712.

96. Polycarp Leyser (1690–1728), *Historia poetarum et poematum medii aevi decem*, . . . *Halae Magdeb* [*urgicae*], 1721. Octavo.

Hroswitha mentioned.

97. Johann Albert Fabricius (1668–1736), *Bibliotheca Latina mediae et infimae aetatis*, 6 vols., Padua, 1754. Quarto.

About Hroswitha, in Vol. 3, pp. 282–284. The author was a German classical scholar and bibliographer. The book was reprinted in 1858.

98. Gottfried Wilhelm von Leibniz (1646–1716), *Operum tomi quarti pars secunda continens opuscula ad historiam et antiquitates pertinentia*, Geneva, 1758. Quarto.

About Hroswitha, p. 5.

99. [Justin Elias Wüstemann,] *Geschichte der Roswitha, eines Stiftsfräuleins von Gandersheim*, [Leipzig,] 1758. Octavo.

82

100. Georg Christoph Hamberger (1726–1773), *Zuverläs-sige Nachrichten von den vornehmsten Schriftstellern vom An-fange der Welt bis 1500*, 4 vols., Lemgo, 1756–1764.

Article on Hroswitha in Vol. 3, 1760, pp. 703–706.

101. Johann Matthias Schröckh (1733–1808), *Abbildungen und Lebensbeschreibungen berühmter Gelehrten*, 2 vols., 2nd ed., Helmstedt, 1766, 1767. Octavo.

"Roswitha, eine Nonne in dem Stifte zu Gandersheim," in Vol. 1, pp. 241–250.

102. [William Hayley] (1745–1820), *A Philosophical, His-torical and Moral Essay on Old Maids*, 3 vols., London, 1785. Octavo.

About Hroswitha, pp. 88–90, in Vol. 3. A second edition was published in 1786, where the Hroswitha material appears on pp. 88–91, also in Vol. 3. The author reports he had been trying to find a copy of Hroswitha's works in various libraries in England without success, and the hoped-for copy from abroad had not arrived in time, so he could not include any of her plays as he had wished to do. But see No. 26, the third edition (1793), where two of the plays were published (in Latin) with Hroswitha's own Preface, translated; in this edition Hroswitha is discussed in Vol. 3, pp. 51–54.

103. Jean-Baptiste Maugérard (1740-1815), "Notice de l'édi-tion originale des oeuvres de Hrotsvite, dont il existe un mag-nifique exemplaire dans la bibliothèque de Mgr. l'archevêque de Toulouse" in *Esprit des journeaux, François et étrangers*, Paris, April, 1788, pp. 257–262. Octavo.

The author was an erudite Benedictine monk.

104. Friedrich Wilken (1777–1840), *Geschichte der Bildung Beraubung und Vernichtung der alten heidelbergischen Bücher-sammlungen*, Heidelberg, 1817.

Page 349 contains information about No. 6, which includes Adam Wernher von Themar's German translation of Hroswitha's *Abraham*. See also No. 183.

105. Theodor Hell, pseud. [Carl Gottfried Theodor Winkler] (1775–1856), "Roswitha: Biographische Skizze," in *Penelope für 1821*, Leipzig, 1821, pp. V–XVI.

106. Engelbert Klüpfel (18th–19th century), *De vita et scriptis Conradi Celtis protucii*, edited by J. C. Ruef and C. Zell, 2 vols., Freiburg i/B, 1827.

A rich store of source materials rather than an organic biography, according to Spitz. The author was an Augustinian monk, professor at Freiburg.

See Nos. 107 and 303.

107. Georg-Philip Schmidt von Lübeck (1766–1849), *Historische Studien*, Altona, 1827.

"Roswitha," pp. 1–58. The author was a German poet.

108. Stephen Ladislaus Endlicher (1804–1849), "Über Klüpfels Werk." Review in *Jahrbücher der Literatur*, Vol. 45, Vienna, 1829, pp. 141 ff.

Includes a list of Celtes' correspondents and the dates and subjects of their letters; these are of importance here in connection with the Aschbach controversy.

See Nos. 106 and 143.

109. Abel François Villemain (1790–1867), *Cours de littérature Française*, 2 vols., Paris, 1829.

Villemain, a French statesman and historian, believed Hroswitha's plays were performed by the young sisters at Gandersheim.

Haraszti, *op. cit.*, p. 101.

110. H. Th. Contzen, *Geschichtsschreiber der sächsischen Kaiserzeit*, Regensburg, 1837.

Hroswitha mentioned pp. 109 ff. The book was also published in Augsburg during that same year, 1837.

111. Gustav Freytag (1816–1895), *De Hrosuitha poetria scripsit et comoediam Abraham inscriptam adjecit*, Breslau, 1839 (dissertation).

The author was a German novelist, historian, dramatist, and poet.

Haraszti, *op. cit.*, p. 101.

112. Victor Euphémion Philarète Chasles (1798–1873), "Théâtre de Hrosvita traduit par M. Charles Magnin," review in *Revue des deux mondes*, Vol. 11, Paris, 1845, pp. 707–731.

113. Victor Euphémion Philarète Chasles, "Hrosvita: Naissance du drame chrétien au Xe siècle," in *Études sur les premiers temps du Christianisme et sur le Moyen Age*, Paris, 1847, pp. 241–279.

The article was reprinted in *Étude sur l'Allemagne ancienne et moderne*, Paris, 1854.

114. Édélstand Pontas Du Méril (1801–1871), *Les origines Latines du théâtre moderne*, Paris, 1849.

Du Méril attacked the theory of Magnin that Hroswitha's plays were produced in her lifetime.

See No. 280, p. 443.

115. Adolphe Napoléon Didron (1806–1867), *Christian Iconography*, translated by E. J. Millington, 2 vols., London, 1851, 1891.

About Hroswitha's *Opera*, 1501 edition (see No. 15), in Vol. 1, pp. 252–253; speaks of a copy in the Bibliothèque Mazarine, and of the beauty of the woodcuts. Didron was a French archaeologist.

116. Johannes Scherr (1817–1886), *Deutsche Kultur- und Sittengeschichte*, Leipzig, 1852.

About Hroswitha, pp. 77–78. The second edition was published in 1858, and a fifth edition in 1873.

Haraszti, *op. cit.*, p. 103.

117. Hippolyte Julien Joseph Lucas (1807–1878), *Curiosités dramatiques et littéraires*, Paris, 1855.

About Hroswitha, pp. 395–406.

118. Ignatius Eduard Dorer-Egloff (1807–1864), *Roswitha, die nonne von Gandersheim*, Aarau, 1857.

See No. 280, p. 444.

119. Anton Ruland (1809–1874), "Der original-codex der Roswitha und die Herausgabe desselben durch Conrad Celtes," in *Serapeum, Zeitschrift für Bibliothekwissenschaft, Handschriftenkunde und ältere Literatur*, Vol. 18, No. 2, Leipzig, 1857, pp. 17–25.

Ruland was a German librarian and politician; this is the first fairly detailed description of No. 1.

Haraszti, *op. cit.*, p. 102; p. 164. See also No. 144.

120. Karl Friederich Adolf Konrad Bartsch (1832–1888), "Die Werke der Hrotsvitha herausgegeben von K. A. Barack," Nürnberg, 1858, review in *Germania*, Vol. 3, Stuttgart, 1858, pp. 375–381.

For Barack's edition of Hroswitha, see No. 36.

121. Franz von Löher (1818–1892), "Hrotsvitha und ihre Zeit," in *Wissenschaftliche Vorträge gehalten zu München, in München, im Winter 1858*, Munich, 1858, p. 484.

122. Ernst Christian Wilhelm Wattenbach (1819–1897), *Deutschlands Geschichtsquellen im Mittelalter bis zur Mitte des dreizehnten Jahrhunderts*, Berlin, 1858.

About Hroswitha, pp. 2, 163, 165, 166, 171, and 172. The author was a famous German paleographer; his book was reprinted in 1885 in two volumes (about Hroswitha in Vol. 1, pp. 313–316), and again in 1938 (about Hroswitha in Vol. 1, pp. 34 ff.).

Haraszti, *op. cit.*, p. 150.

123. Mikhail Kublitskii (1821–1875), *Literaturnaya mozaika* (*Literary Mosaic*), Leipzig, 1860.

About Hroswitha, pp. 20–46. The author was a Russian musicologist and connoisseur of drama.

124. Jane Williams (1806–1885), *The Literary Women of England*, London, 1861.

Reference to Hroswitha, pp. 20–21. The author was a Welsh poet.

125. Albert Cohn (1827–1905), *Shakespeare in Germany in the Sixteenth and Seventeenth Centuries*, London, 1865.

About Hroswitha and the similarity of some of her dramatic lines to those of Shakespeare, in Chapter I, pp. I–II.

126. Ferencz Toldy (1805–1875), *Geschichte der ungarischen Literatur im Mittelalter*, translated into German by Moritz Kolbenheyer, Budapest, 1865.

The Hungarian edition of this work, *Az ó- és középkori magyar nemzeti irodalom története*, in two volumes, appeared in 1862. Page 262 of the German edition contains a description of Hroswitha's "Dulcitius" translated into Hungarian as it appeared in the *Sándor*

Codex; Toldy was the first to describe this text but he did not recognize it as one of Hroswitha's and merely listed it as "Legenden der h. Agape, Ciona, und Irene."

See Nos. 7 and 178.

127. Joseph von Aschbach (1801–1882), "Anzeige Roswitha und Conrad Celtes," in *Serapeum*, Leipzig, 1867, pp. 317–320.

The author was an Austrian historian.

128. Joseph von Aschbach, "Roswitha und Conrad Celtes," in *Kaiserlichen Akademie der Wissenschaften Wien, Philosophisch-historische Klasse, Sitzungsberichte*, Vol. 56, Vienna, 1867, pp. 3–62.

This lecture was given by Aschbach before the Academy's section of philosophy and history on May 8, 1867. In it Aschbach declared that Hroswitha's works were forgeries; that they were written by Conrad Celtes and his friends of the Sodalitas Rhenana; and that the whole fraud was perpetrated for the glorification of German history and literature.

Haraszti, *op. cit.*, pp. 88 ff. See also Nos. 129 and 132.

129. Joseph von Aschbach, *Roswitha und Conrad Celtes*, Vienna, aus der K. K. Hof und Staatsdruckerei, 1867.

A separate printing in pamphlet form, 64 pages.

See also Nos. 128 and 132.

130. Ernst Rudolf Anastasius Köpke (1813–1870), *Widukind von Korvei, ein Beitrag zur Kritik der Geschichtsschreiber des X Jahrhunderts* (Series title: *Ottonische Studien zur deutschen Geschichte im zehnten Jahrhundert. I*), Berlin, 1867.

Widukind, as one of the better known of the X-century writers, is important for background material in any study of Hroswitha's works.

131. Georg Waitz (1813–1886), "Roswitha und Conrad Celtes von Joseph Aschbach," review in *Göttingische Gelehrte Anzeigen*, Vol. 2, August 7, 1867, Göttingen, pp. 1261–1270.

A refutation of Aschbach by a noted German historian.

Haraszti, *op. cit.*, p. 111.

132. Joseph von Aschbach, *Roswitha und Conrad Celtes*, Enlarged edition, Vienna, 1868.

In this book of 119 pages, Aschbach tries to reply to some of his critics.

Haraszti, *op. cit.*, pp. 88–113; pp. 139–173.

133. Élie Petit, "Théâtre de Hrotswitha," in *Revue de l'art Chrétien*, Vol. 12, Paris, 1868, pp. 5–23.

A discussion of Hroswitha's plays.

134. Anton Ruland, "Roswitha und Conrad Celtes von Joseph Aschbach. 2 vermehrte Auflage," review in *Theologisches Literaturblatt*, Bonn, 1868, columns 55–62 and 101–105.

135. Aleksandr Ivanovich Kirpichnikov (1845–1903), *Ocherki iz istorii srednevekovot literatury* (*Essays in the History of Medieval Literature*), Moscow, 1869.

About Hroswitha, pp. 247–254: "Hroswitha's literary work constitutes a strange phenomenon. Her comedies stand isolated; neither before nor after is there anything similar. They did not originate in the Church as the mediaeval mysteries did, nor do they belong to the miracles, but arise from the classical ground . . . ; as drama they are superior to the French mysteries that developed in the XIII and XIV centuries." These comments are followed by a biographical summary, mostly based on Barack, a list of her works with short summaries, and excerpts from *Gallicanus* and *Dulcitius* in a Russian translation. The article concludes with the statement: "Hroswitha's dramas are dialoguized lives of the Saints . . . It is not known whether they were played in monastical theaters." [Translation from the Russian, and summary, by Dr. Marek Waysblum, London, 1961.]

Kirpichnikov was a well-known Russian historian whose work is found in all of the larger Russian libraries and also in the British Museum.

136. Ernst Rudolf Anastasius Köpke, *Die älteste deutsche Dichterin*, Berlin, 1869.

A biography of Hroswitha.

137. Ernst Rudolf Anastasius Köpke, *Hrotsuit von Gandersheim* (Series title: *Ottonische Studien zur deutschen Geschichte im zehnten Jahrhundert*, II), Berlin, 1869.

An important refutation of Aschbach's claim that No. 1 was a forgery by Conrad Celtes and his friends (see Nos. 128 and 132).

Illustrations. One folding plate containing a reproduction of No. 1, folio 63 (8 lines); folio 80 (8 lines); and folio 133 (6 lines, with 4 lines added in another hand).

Haraszti, *op. cit.*, pp. 141–148.

138. Élie Petit, "Les poèmes latins de Hrotswitha," in *Revue de l'art chrétien*, Vol. 13, Paris, 1869, pp. 81–96 and 134–153.

A discussion of Hroswitha's poems.

139. Georg Waitz, "Über das Verhältnis von Hrotsuits Gesta Oddonis zu Widukind," in *Forschungen zur deutschen Geschichte*, Vol. 9, Göttingen, 1869, pp. 335–342.

140. Karl Friederich Adolf Konrad Bartsch, "Zur Hrotswithfrage," in *Germania*, Vol. 15, Vienna, 1870, p. 194.

141. Guillaume Alfred Heinrich (1829–1887), "Notice sur le théâtre de Hrotswitha," in *Histoire de la littérature Allemande*, 3 vols., Paris, 1870–1873, Vol. 1, pp. 60–73, 261–262, and 403; and Vol. 2, pp. 566–567.

142. A. Pannenborg, "Über den Ligurinus," in *Forschungen zur deutschen Geschichte*, Vol. 11, Göttingen, 1871, pp. 163–300.

Concerning the authenticity of the Ligurinus manuscript, which was also supposed to have been forged by Celtes and thus had bearing on Aschbach's claim against the Hroswitha manuscript, No. 1.

Haraszti, *op. cit.*, pp. 151–153 (Haraszti identifies Pannenborg as a pupil of Georg Waitz's).

143. Ernst Christian Wilhelm Wattenbach, "Die Ehrenrettung des Ligurinus," in *Historische Zeitschrift*, Vol. 26, Munich, 1871, pp. 386–400.

Hroswitha is briefly mentioned, but all reasoning on the Ligurinus manuscript is of importance to a study of the Aschbach controversy about the Hroswitha manuscript.

144. Vasilii Aleksyeyevich Bilbasov (1838–1904), "Monakhina Rosvita, pisatel'nitza X viecka" ("The nun Hroswitha, writer of the tenth century"), in *Zhurnal ministerstva narodnogo prosviasccheniia*, *SPB* (*Journal of the Ministry of Education, SPB*), part 167, Div. of Science, St. Petersburg (Leningrad), 1873, pp. 1–28 and 211–259.

A scholarly refutation of Aschbach, based on a first-hand study of No. 1 and a review of most of the basic reference material, ancient and contemporary. [This note is based on an English summary of Bilbasov's article made for the Hroswitha Club through the courtesy of Mrs. Nathalie Scheffer.]

Bilbasov was a brilliant scholar and prolific Russian historian, some of whose works are available at the New York Public Library.

145. Moritz Haupt (1808–1874), "Coniectanae," in *Hermes: Zeitschrift für klassische Philologie*, Vol. 7, Berlin, 1873.

Hroswitha mentioned, pp. 189–190.

146. Hugo Franz Philipp Wilder von Walderdorff (1829–1918), *Hrotsuit von Gandersheim* (lecture, revised), [Place?] 1873.

This lecture was given in 1869, but no record has been found of its publication before 1873. It was republished in the *Historischen Vereins von Oberpfalz und Regensburg, Verhandlungen*, Vol. 29 (N.F. 21), Regensburg, 1874, pp. 89–105.

147. Julius Leopold Klein (1810–1876), *Geschichte des Dramas*, Vol. 3: *Des ausser-europäischen Dramas und der lateinischen Schauspiele nach Christus bis Ende des X Jahrhunderts*, Leipzig, 1874.

About Hroswitha, pp. 648 ff. Klein was a Hungarian-born German poet and dramatist. The work was reprinted in 1886.

See Nos. 208, p. 116, and 280, p. 444.

148. Wilhelm Scherer (1841–1886), *Geschichte der deutschen Literatur des 11. und 12. Jahrhunderts*, Strassburg, 1875.

The book contains a mention of Hroswitha's works; it was reprinted in Berlin in 1883. The author was an Austrian-born German philologist, professor successively at Vienna, Strassburg, and Berlin; *Geschichte* is one of his best-known works.

See No. 280, p. 444.

149. Bruno Zint (1851–?), *Über Roswitha's Carmen de Gestis Oddonis* (Dissertation der Philosophischen Fakultät, Königsberg), Tiegenhof (i.e., Nowy Dwor Gdanski, Poland), [1875].

150. Karl Hartfelder (1848–1893), "Wernher von Themar, ein Heidelberger Humanist," in *Zeitschrift für die Geschichte des Oberrheins*, Vol. 33, Karlsruhe, 1880, pp. 1–101.

Wernher von Themar made the first German translation of Hroswitha's *Abraham* in 1503 (see No. 6).

See No. 183, pp. 45–46.

151. L. Loparco, "Il Gallicano di Rosvita e il Martirio dei Sancti Giovanni e Paolo di Lorenzo il Magnifico" in *Una commedia Latina del secolo X e una sacra rappresentazione del secolo XV*, Naples, 1880.

152. L. Ruberto, "Il Gallicanus di Rosvita e il San Giovanni e Paolo di Lorenzo il Magnifico," in *Giornale Napoletano de filosofia e lettere*, Anno II, New Series Vol. 4, Naples, 1880, pp. 123–133.

153. Sándor Szilágyi (1829–1899), *Catalogus codicum bibliothecae universitatis Reg. Scientiarum*, Budapest, 1881.

Catalogue description on pp. 119–120 of *Codex Hungaricus Universitatis Budapestinensis 6* (known as the *Sándor Codex*), which includes a Hungarian translation of Hroswitha's *Dulcitius*; the manuscript is dated early XVI century (see No. 7).

154. R. Steinhoff, "Hrosvitha . . . die älteste deutsche Dichterin," in *Zeitschrift des Harz-Vereins für Geschichte und Alterthumskunde*, Wernigerode, 1882, pp. 116–140.

155. Karl Friederick Ludwig Gödeke (1814–1887), *Grundrisz zur Geschichte der deutschen Dichtung aus den Quellen, Vol. 1: Das Mittelalter*, 2nd ed., Dresden, 1884.

Bibliography of Hroswitha's works, p. 32.

156. Enrico Panzacchi (1841–1904), "Hroswitha," in *Fanfulla della Domenica*, March 22, 1885.

157. Otto Grashof (1812–1876), "Das Benedictinerinnenstift Gandersheim und Hrotsuitha, die Zierde des Benedictinerordens," in *Studien und Mitteilungen aus dem Benedictiner- und dem Cistercienser-Orden*, Vol. 6, Salzburg, 1885, pp. 303–322; Vol. 7, Salzburg, 1886, pp. 87–109, and 393-406.

158. Enrico Panzacchi, "Suora Hrosvita," in *Critica spicciola*, Rome, 1886, pp. 243–259.

This article was reprinted in *Saggi Critici*, Naples, 1896, pp. 243–255.

159. Marie Adrien Perk (1834–1916), *De tonneelarbeid eener non uit de teinde eeuw* (*The Dramatic Works of a Nun of the Tenth Century*), Amsterdam, 1886.

The author was a Dutch divine.

160. Adolf Ebert (1820–1890), *Allegemeine Geschichte der Literatur des Mittelalters im Abendlande*, 3 vols., Leipzig, 1874–1887.

Article about Hroswitha in Vol. 3 (1887), pp. 285–329.

161. O. Holder-Egger, "Aus Münchener Handschriften," in *Gesellschaft für ältere deutsche Geschichtskunde, Neues Archiv*, Vol. 13, Hanover, 1888, pp. 573–574, and 577.

Mentions No. 4, with a description of its contents, but fails to note Hroswitha's name as the author of *Gallicanus*, included in the manuscript.

162. William Henry Hudson (1841–1922), "Hrosvitha of Gandersheim," in *English Historical Review*, Vol. 3, London, July, 1888, pp. 431–459.

Haraszti, *op. cit.*, pp. 155–156.

163. Anatole France, pseud. [Jacques Anatole Franc Thibault] (1844–1924), "Les marionnettes de M. Signoret," and "Hroswitha aux marionnettes," in *Le Temps*, June 10, 1888; and April 7, 1889.

"Hroswitha aux marionnettes" was reprinted in *La vie littéraire*, Vol. 3, Paris [*c.* 1891], pp. 10–19, and both articles appeared in *Oeuvres complètes*, Paris, 1926, in Vol. 6, pp. 464–468, and Vol. 7, pp. 23–31.

164. Enrico Panzacchi, "Monaca e romanziere," in *Lettere e arti*, Anno I, No. 33, Bologna, 1889.

165. Otto Schmid (1858–1931), "Roswitha von Gandersheim," in *Allgemeine deutsche Biographie*, Vol. 29, Leipzig, 1889, pp. 283–294.

There is a good Hroswitha bibliography included on pp. 292–294. The author was a German musicologist.

166. Wilhelm Cloetta (1857–1911), *Beiträge zur Literaturgeschichte des Mittelalters und der Renaissance, I: Komödie und Tragödie im Mittelalter*, Halle, 1890.

Hroswitha mentioned pp. 127 and 163.

See No. 280, p. 445.

167. Ellen Fries (1855–1900), *Märkvärdiga qvinnor: Utländka qvinnor* (*Remarkable Women: Foreign Women*), Stockholm, 1890.

Article on Hroswitha, pp. 3–18. The author was a Swedish biographer and historian.

168. [Aglauro Ungherini] (1847–?), *Manuel de bibliographie biographique et d'iconographie des femmes célèbres*, Turin, 1892.

About Hroswitha, pp. 354–355. A supplement was printed in 1900, with Hroswitha material appearing on p. 239.

169. Wilhelm Michael Anton Creizenach (1851–1919), *Geschichte des neueren Dramas, Vol. 1: Mittelalter und Frührenaissance*, Halle, 1893.

Hroswitha mentioned pp. 17–20. Creizenach believed that Hroswitha's plays were not intended for acting. *Geschichte* was republished in Halle in 1919, with Hroswitha material appearing on pp. 3, 16–19, and 510.

See No. 280, p. 445.

170. Gyula Zolnai (1862–?), *Nyelvemlékeink a könyvyomtatás koráig* (*Our Linguistic Records Up to the Age of Printing*), Budapest, 1894.

Contains a description of the early XVI-century Hungarian *Sándor Codex*, but has no mention of the Hroswitha *Dulcitius* contained therein; includes a bibliography of other Hungarian works dealing with the *Sándor Codex* (see No. 8).

171. Emil von Ottenthal (1855–?), "Hrosvitha's Ottolied übersetzt . . . von W. Gundlach," review in *Mitteilungen des Instituts für Österreichische Geschichte*, Vol. 16, 1895, pp. 357–360.

For Gundlach's translation see No. 41.

172. Lina Eckenstein (*d.* 1931), "The nun Hroswitha and her writings," in *Women Under Monasticism*, Cambridge, 1896, pp. 160–183.

173. Emma Boghen Conigliani, "Hroswitha," in *Studi letterari,* Rocca San Casciano, Capelli, 1897, pp. 233–242.

174. Harry Bresslau (1848-1926), *Bodo's Syntagma de constructione coenobii Gandesiani und die darin uberlieferten Kaiserurkunden in Gesellschaft für ältere deutsche Geschichtskunde, Neues Archiv,* Vol. 23, Hanover, 1898, pp. 134–145.

This is a study of the manuscript of Bodo's *Syntagma,* which appears on leaves 1–71 of No. 10, and other *Syntagma* manuscripts; see No. 18.

175. Enrico Panzacchi, *Morti e vivanti,* Catania, 1898.

About Hroswitha, pp. 128–139.

176. Paul Karl Rudolf von Winterfeld (1872–1905), "Zu Hrotsvits Theophilus v. 17," in *Zeitschrift für deutsches Altertum und deutsche Literatur,* Vol. 43, Berlin, 1899, pp. 45–46.

177. Otto von Heinemann (1824–1904), *Die Handschriften der Herzoglichen Bibliothek zu Wolfenbüttel: Zweite Abteilung, Die Augusteischen Handschriften IV,* Wolfenbüttel, 1900.

Contains a description of Bodo's *Syntagma* as it appears in No. 10, p. 267, and in No. 18.

The author was a German bibliographer.

178. L. Katona, "Die altungarische Übersetzung des Dulcitius der Hrotsuitha," in *Allgemeine Zeitung,* Beilage No. 123, Munich, May, 1900, pp. 6–7.

Katona was the first to recognize this as a Hroswitha text; he reported his discovery at a conference of the Budapest Philological Society, May 12, 1899, and it was first published in *Allgemeine Zeitung,* as given above.

Zeydel, *op. cit.,* III–20. See also No. 7.

179. Arthur J. Roberts (1867–1927), "Did Hrotswitha imitate Terence?" in *Modern Language Notes*, Vol. 16, Baltimore, Md., 1901, columns 478–481 (see also a critical note on this article by J. M. Hart of Cornell University, in *Modern Language Notes*, Vol. 17, 1902, column 463).

Roberts was associated with Colby College, Waterville, Maine.

180. F. Hirsch, "Hrotsvithae opera, recensuit et emendavit Paul de Winterfeld," review in *Historische Gesellschaft: Mitteilungen aus der historischen Literatur*, Vol. 30, Berlin, 1902, pp. 408–409.

For Winterfeld's work see No. 43.

181. M. M. . . . s., "Hrotsvithae opera, recensuit et emendavit Paulus de Winterfeld," review in *Literarisches Centralblatt für Deutschland*, Vol. 53, Leipzig, 1902, columns 1533–1534.

For Winterfeld's work see No. 43.

182. Karl Strecker (1861–1933), *Hrotsvits Maria und Pseudo-Matthaeus* (Programm, Gymnasium zu Dortmund, Jahrgang 1901–1902), Dortmund, 1902.

183. Jakob Wille (1853–?), *Katalog der Handschriften der Universitätsbibliothek in Heidelberg, Vol. 2: Die deutschen Pfalzer Handschriften des 16. und 17. Jahrhunderts*, Heidelberg, 1903.

On pp. 45 and 46 there is a description of No. 6 which includes Adam Wernher von Themar's German translation of Hroswitha's *Abraham*.

184. Albert Ostheide, "Hrotsvit von Gandersheim," in *Deutsche Heimat Blätter für Literatur und Volkstum*, Vol. 39, Leipzig and Berlin, 1903, pp. 1317–1328.

185. Karl Strecker, "Hrotsvit von Gandersheim," in *Neue Jahrbücher für das klassische Altertum Geschichte und deutsche Literatur, und für Pädegogik*, Jahrgang 6 [Vol. 11], Leipzig, 1903, pp. 569–596, and 629–647.

186. Valentin Rose, *Verzeichnisse der lateinischen Handschriften*, Vol. 2, part 3 (Series title: *Handschriftenverzeichnisse der Königlichen Bibliothek zu Berlin*, Band 13, Vol. 2, part 3), Berlin, 1905.

    About No. 8, pp. 1283–1284.

187. Paul Karl Rudolf von Winterfeld, "Hrosvits literarische Stellung," in *Archiv für das Studium der neueren Sprachen und Literaturen*, Vol. 114 (N.F. Vol. 14), Brunswick, 1905, pp. 25–75, and 293–325.

    This article was reprinted in No. 47.

188. Karl Strecker, *Textkritisches zu Hrotsvit* (Programm, Gymnasium zu Dortmund, Jahrgang 1905–1906), Dortmund, 1906.

189. Bernarda Trümper, *Hrotsuithas Frauen-Gestalten*, Münster, 1908.

190. Frances Reubelt (1869–?), *Hrotswith and Terence* (thesis, A.M., University of Chicago, 1909, typewritten).

    There is one leaf of bibliography at the end.

191. Alice Kemp-Welch (Mrs. W.), "A tenth-century dramatist: Roswitha the nun," in *The Nineteenth Century and After*, Vol. 66, No. 393, New York and London, November, 1909, pp. 814–826.

See also No. 200.

192. Paul Lehmann (1884–?), "Nachrichten von der Sponheimer Bibliothek des Abtes Joh. Tritheimius," in *Festgabe für H. Gauert*, Freiburg i/B, 1910, pp. 205–220.

Tritheim was a friend of Conrad Celtes and was the first person to mention Hroswitha's works in print (see No. 78). Paul Lehmann was a German bibliographer.

193. Philip Schuyler Allen (1871–1937), "The mediaeval mimus, Part II," in *Modern Philology*, Vol. 8, No. 1, Chicago, 1910–1911, pp. 17–44 (including "Mimus" and "Roswitha," pp. 23–29).

The author was an editor and philologist.

194. Dr. L. Simons, *"Hrotsvitha en Waltharius,"* in *Koniklijke Vlaamsche Academie vor Taal-en Letterkunde, Verslagen en Mededeelingen*, Ghent, 1911, pp. 452–453, and 457–478.

195. Maximilianus Manitius (1853–1933), *Geschichte der lateinischen Literatur des Mittelalters* (Series title: *Handbuch der Altertumswissenschaft*), 3 vols. Munich, 1911–1931.

About Hroswitha, in Vol. 1, pp. 619–632, and in Vol. 3, p. 1064.

196. Johann Schneiderhan, *Roswitha von Gandersheim, die erste deutsche Dichterin*, Paderborn, 1912.

197. P. Ambros Sturm, "Das Quadrivium in den Dichtungen Roswithas von Gandersheim," in *Studien und Mitteilungen zur Geschichte des Benediktiner-Ordens und seiner Zeit*, Vol. 33 (N.F. Vol. 2), Salzburg, 1912, pp. 332–338.

For a review of this by Karl Strecker, see No. 199.

198. Rémy de Gourmont (1858–1915), *Le Latin mystique*. Paris, 1913.

About Hroswitha, pp. 104–105.

199. Karl Strecker, "Das Quadrivium in Dichtungen Roswithas, von P. A. Sturm," review in *Gesellschaft für ältere deutsche Geschichtskunde, Neues Archiv*, Vol. 38, Hanover, 1913, p. 390.

For Sturm's article, see No. 197.

200. Alice Kemp-Welch (Mrs. W.), "A tenth-century dramatist, Roswitha the nun," in *Of Six Mediaeval Women*, London, 1913, pp. 1–28.

First printed as a magazine article in 1909 (see No. 191).

See No. 208, p. 117.

201. Darley Dale, pseud. [Francesca Maria Steele], "Roswitha, nun and dramatist," in *The American Catholic Quarterly Review*, Vol. 39, No. 155, Philadelphia, July 1914, pp. 442–457.

202. Mikhail Matveyevich Stasyulebich (1826–1911), "Monakhinya Rosvita: Iz poemy ob Ottone Velikkom, 949–952," ("The Nun Hroswitha: From the poem about Otto the Great, 949–952"), in *Istoriya srednickh vekov v yeie sisatelyakh i issledovaniyakh noveishikh uchenykh* (*History of the Middle Ages, as Represented in the Period's Writers and Latest Scientists' Research*), 2 vols., 4th ed., Petersburg, 1913–1915, Vol. 2, 1915, pp. 457–463.

The study is based on the text published in No. 29. *Istoriya* was first published in three volumes in 1863–1865; the last edition of Vol. 3 was 1907; the 4th edition reprinted Vols. 1 and 2. The author was a noted Russian historian.

203. Aleksandr L'vovich Pogodin (1872–?), *Zapiski po istorii zapadno-evropeiskikh literatur . . .* (*Notes on the History of Western European Literatures . . .*), Krakow, 1916.

About Hroswitha, pp. 32 and 35.

204. Evangeline Wilbour Blashfield (Mrs. E. H.) (*d.* 1918), *Portraits and Backgrounds*, New York, 1917.

About Hroswitha, pp. 3–112, including excerpts of all the plays translated into English, with a study of their dramatic qualities. The author was an American woman of letters.

205. Gustav Roethe (1859–1926), *Vom Altertum zur Gegenwart, die Kulturzusammenhange in der Hauptepochen und auf der Hauptgebieten: Literatur*, Leipzig and Berlin, 1919.

About Hroswitha, p. 156. The author was a Polish-born teacher of German philology.

206. P. K. Sommer, "Albrecht Dürer und Roswitha von Gandersheim," in *Gartenlaube*, Vol. 69, Leipzig and Berlin, 1921, pp. 675–676.

207. Goswin Frenken (1887–), "Eine neue Hrotsvithhandschrift," in *Gesellschaft für ältere deutsche Geschichtskunde*, *Neues Archiv*, Vol. 44, Hanover, 1922, pp. 101–114.

Concerning the discovery of No. 2.

Haraszti, *op. cit.*, pp. 161–164; Zeydel, *op. cit.*, II–4.

208. Oswald Robert Kuehne, *A study of the Thaïs legend, with special reference to Hroswitha's Paphnutius*, Philadelphia, Pa., 1922 (thesis, Ph. D., University of Pennsylvania, 1922).

Bibliography on pp. 116–117.

See No. 211 for a review of this work.

209. William A. Drake (1899–?), "Roswitha of Gandersheim," in *Texan Review*, Vol. 8, Austin, Texas, 1923, pp. 257–272.

210. Paul Alpers (1887–), "Hrotsvit von Gandersheidiem, erste niedersächsische Dichterin," in *Niedersachsen*, Vol. 29, Bremen, 1924, pp. 302–306.

211. Edward Schroeder (1858–1942), "A study of the Thaïs legend with special reference to Hrotsvitha's Paphnutius, by Oswald R. Kuehne," review in *Anzeiger für deutsches Altertum*, Vol. 43, Berlin, 1924, p. 31.

The author was a German philologist. For Kuehne's work see No. 208.

212. Konrad Burdach (1859–1936), *Vorspiel: Gesammelte Schriften zur Geschichte des deutschen Geistes* (Series title: *Deutsche Vierteljahrschrift für Literaturwissenschaft und Geistesgeschichte*, Series 1: *Mittelalter*, Part 1), Halle, 1925.

About Hroswitha, pp. 137–139. The author was a German scholar and philologist.

213. George Raleigh Coffman (1880–1958), "A new approach to Medieval Latin drama," in *Modern Philology*, Vol. 22, Chicago, 1925, pp. 230–271 (includes "Hrotswitha the poetess of Gandersheim," pp. 261–264).

The author was an American dramaturgist.

214. Boris Isaakovich Jarcho [in Russian: Yarkho], (1889– ?), "Stilquellen der Hrotsvitha," in *Zeitschrift für deutsches Altertum und deutsche Literatur*, Vol. 62 (New Series Vol. 50), Berlin, 1925, pp. 236–240.

Jarcho was a Russian medievalist and professor of the theory of poetry. He points out that Hroswitha created her firmly constructed and fluent dialogue not only from Terence, but also from elements of the living school-and-church language of the period; much of it was probably derived from Alcuin, whose textbooks on grammar and rhetoric were written in dialogue style and formed a basic part of the school of literature of the Carolingian Age and later.

The Hroswitha Club of New York has the typescript of an English translation of the article, done for the Club by Hellmut Lehmann-Haupt.

215. Hermann Menhardt (1888–?), "Eine unbekannte Hrots-vitha-Handschrift," in *Zeitschrift für deutsches Altertum und deutsche Literatur*, Vol. 62 (New Series Vol. 50), Berlin, 1925, pp. 233–236.

A description of No. 3.
The Hroswitha Club of New York has the typescript of an English translation of the article, done for the Club by Hellmut Lehmann-Haupt.

Haraszti, *op. cit.*, pp. 161–164.

216. Sister M. Hilda Obermeier (1893–), *Hrotsuitha, Gandersheim, and the Saxon house*, probably unpublished (thesis, M.A., Catholic University of America, 1925).

217. K. Polcheim, *Die lateinische Reimprosa*, Berlin, 1925.

About Hroswitha, pp. 504–509, including a bibliography.

218. Karl Brandi (1868–1946), "Hrotsvit von Gandersheim," in *Deutsche Rundschau*, Vol. 209, Berlin, 1926, pp. 247–260.

219. Karl Brandi, "Zur Tausendjahrfeier von Gandersheim: Sachsen und die Dichtung Hrotsvits," in *Braunschweigisches Magazin*, Vol. 32, Wolfenbüttel, 1926, pp. 81–92.

220. Susanne Hoffman, "Tausendjahrfeier zu Gandersheim," in *Braunschweigische Heimat*, Vol. 17, Braunschwieg, 1926, pp. 82–84.

221. Friedrich Röse, "Von der Tausendjährigen Hrotswitha-Stadt Gandersheim," in *Illustrierte Zeitung*, Vol. 166, Leipzig, June 24, 1926, p. 866.

222. Bruno Vignola (1878–1957?), "Rosvita," in *La cultura: Rivista mensile di filosofia, lettere, arte*, Vol. 6, Rome, 1926–1927, pp. 307–310.

223. Filippo Ermini (1868–1935), "Le opere di Hrosvitha," in *Nuova antologia*, Vol. 329, Rome, 1927, pp. 453–458.

A critical article on Hroswitha's works.

224. Ivo Fischer, "Der Nachlass des Abtes Trithemius von St. Jakob in Würzburg," in *Historischer Verein von Unterfranken und Aschaffenburg, Archiv*, Vol. 67, Würzburg, 1928, pp. 41–82.

225. Boris Isaakovitch Jarcho [in Russian: Yarkho], "Zu Hrosvithas Wirkungskreis," in *Speculum, a Journal of Mediaeval Studies*, Vol. 2, No. 3, Boston, Mass., July, 1927, pp. 343–344.

The relation of "Vita Mathildis Reginae II" to Hroswitha's work.

226. Hermann Menhardt, ed., *Handschriftenverzeichnis der Kärtner Bibliotheken* (Series title: *Handschriftenverzeichnisse Österreichischer Bibliotheken*, Vol. 1), Vienna, 1927.

Page 99 contains a description of No. 3.

227. Helen Waddell (1889–), *The Wandering Scholars*. London, 1927.

About Hroswitha, pp. 83–86. There is another edition of the same title published in Boston and New York, 1927; in this the lines about Hroswitha appear on pp. 76–79. The author is a famous Irish medievalist.

228. Bonaventura Tecchi (1896–), "Rosvita," in *Fiera letteraria*, Milan and Rome, April 22, 1928, p. 7.

229. Paul Burg, pseud. [Paul Erich Bruno Richard Schaumburg] (1884–), "Roswitha von Gandersheim: Zur tausendsten Wiederkehr des Geburtstages der ersten deutschen Dichterin," in *Harz: Monatsschrift des Harz-klubs*, Magdeburg, 1929, pp. 204–205.

230. Cornelia Catlin Coulter (1885–), "The 'Terentian' comedies of a tenth-century nun," in *Classical Journal*, Vol. 24, London, 1929, pp. 515–529.

231. F. Reinicke, "Roswitha-Tag in Gandersheim," in *Börsenblatt für den deutschen Buchhandel*, Leipzig, February 27, 1929.

232. Harry Ezekiel Wedeck, "The humour of Hrotsvitha, a medieval nun," in *Humour in Varro and Other Essays*, Oxford, 1929, pp. 75–79.

233. Rosamond Gilder, "Hrotsvitha, the strong voice of Gandersheim," in *Theatre Arts Monthly*, Vol. 14, No. 4, New York and London, April, 1930, pp. 331–344.

The author is a noted American drama critic and editor.

234. Raph Kreemers, "Roswitha, een toneelschrijfster von 1,000 jaar terug," in *Toneelgids*, Vol. 16, pts. 11–12, Leuven, 1930, pp. 161–171.

235. Filippo Ermini, "Il teatro e la Latinità di Hrotsvitha per M. Rigobon," review of inaugural dissertation in *Studi Medievali*, New Series, Vol. 4, 1931, pp. 372–373.

For Rigobon's dissertation see No. 246.

236. Goswin Frenken, "Rezension der Streckerschen Hrots-with-Ausgabe," Review in *Deutsche Literaturzeitung*, Leipzig, June 21, 1931, column 1166.

For Strecker's work see No. 65.

237. Rosamond Gilder, "Hrotsvitha, a tenth-century nun—The first woman playwright," in *Enter the Actress, the First Women in the Theatre*, Boston and New York, 1931, pp. 18–45.

238. Raoul Gout (1879–?), "Anatole France et le théâtre de Hrotsvitha: Une source de Thaïs," in *Mercure de France*, Vol. 209, Paris, 1931, pp. 595–611.

Illustrations. Reproduction of two of the woodcuts from No. 15: Hroswitha presenting her book to Otto, and Calimachus at Druisiana's tomb.

239. János Horvath (1878–?), *Irodalmi müveltségünk kezdetei* (*The Origins of our Literary Education*), Budapest, 1931.

Pages 178 and 233–234 deal with various early XVI-century Hungarian manuscripts, including Hroswitha's *Dulcitius* as it appeared in the *Sándor Codex*. Horvath says: "The glory of the ... *Sándor Codex* is the dialogue of the 'Three Christian Maidens' adapted from the *Dulcitius* of Hroswitha ... the first dramatic play in Hungarian." (For the *Sándor Codex* see No. 7.) The Hroswitha Club of New York has the typescript of an English translation of this article, prepared by János Scholz.

240. Anton Mayer, "Der Heilige und die Dirne: Eine Motivgeschichtliche Studie zu Hrotsvits Abraham und Paphnutius," in *Bayerische Blätter für das Gymnasialschulwesen*, Vol. 67, Munich and Berlin, 1931, pp. 73–98.

241. Luise Bertold [or Berthold] (1891–), "Hrotsviths

Charakter," in *Zeitschrift für deutsche Bildung*, Frankfurt, 1932, pp. 357–361.

The author is a German philologist.

242. Hermann Herbst, *Das Benediktinerkloster Klus bei Gandersheim und die Bursfelder Reform*, Leipzig, 1932.

Description of No. 10, which includes Bodo's *Syntagma*.

243. Edmund E. Tolk, untitled article (65 pages), accompanying Tolk's transcription of the XVI-century manuscript of *Abraham*, translated into German by Adam Wernher von Themar (see No. 6) (unpublished).

Dr. Tolk's transcription is a manuscript of 22 leaves, some on both sides of the sheet, plus one page typed, with manuscript notes on its verso. The transcription and the article were both prepared by Dr. Tolk at Heidelberg in 1932; they are the author's property. Dr. Tolk is Head, Department of German, Manhattan College, New York.

244. "Hroswitha's abbey," in *The Tablet, a Catholic weekly*, Vol. 159, Brooklyn, N. Y., 1932, p. 608.

245. E[mma] Miriam Lone (1872–1953),'Some bookwomen of the fifteenth century," in *The Colophon*, Part 11, New York, 1932, pp. [?] (this volume is without pagination; the article is on the last 8 pages of Part 11).

The article includes mention of Hroswitha as a book-collector and writer of plays.

Illustration. One woodcut reproduced from No. 15: Hroswitha kneeling and presenting her book to Otto the Great.

246. Marcella Rigobon, *Il teatro e la Latinità di Hrotsvitha* (Series title: *R. Università di Padova. Publicazioni della facoltà di lettere e filosofia*, Vol. 2). (Inaugural dissertation, Padua, 1929), Padua, 1932.

First published edition; includes mention of the XVI-century Hungarian translation of *Dulcitius*. For a review of this dissertation see Nos. 235 and 250.

247. Gerald Groveland Walsh, S. J. (1892–), "The loud cry of Gandersheim," in *America*, Vol. 46, New York, March 5, 1932, pp. 531–533.

The author is an American Catholic priest, professor of medical history.

248. Barbara Barclay Carter, "Roswitha of Gandersheim," in *The Dublin Review*, No. 385, London, April, 1933, pp. 284–295.

249. Emma Miriam Lone, "A short sketch of the life and works of Hroswitha, the nun-poetess," in *The American Book-Collector*, Vol. 4, No. 6, Metuchen, N. J., December, 1933, pp. 297–303.

250. B. G. Pighi (1898–), "Il teatro e la Latinità di Hrotsvitha per M. Rigobon," review in *Aevum*, Vol. 7, 1933, pp. 519–520.

For Rigobon's book see No. 246.

251. Karl Young (1879–1943), *The Drama of the Medieval Church*, 2 vols., Oxford, 1933.

About Hroswitha, Vol. I, pp. 2–6, and p. 543 (bibliography). The author was an American professor of English and a dramaturgist.

252. Sebastian Euringer, "Drei Beiträge zur Roswitha-Forschung: Zum 1,000 Geburtstag der ersten deutschen Dichterin," in *Historisches Jahrbuch der Görresgesellschaft*, Vol. 54, Cologne, 1934, pp. 75–83.

253. Robert Stanley Forsythe (1886–), "Terentius Christianus: Hrotsvitha," in *Notes and Queries for Readers and Writers, Collectors and Librarians*, Vol. 169, London, 1935, pp. 443–444.

254. John Heard (1889–), "Hrotsvitha, the nun of Gandersheim, A.D. 930? 935?–1005?" in *Poet Lore*, Vol. 42, Spring Issue, Boston, 1935, pp. 291–298.

255. Walter Stach, "Deutsche Dichtung im lateinischen Gewande: Eine Problembetrachtung," in *Neue Jahrbücher für Wissenschaft und Jugendbildung*, Vol. 11, Leipzig and Berlin, 1935, pp. 343–355.

Many references to Hroswitha.

256. Walter Stach, "Die Gongolf-Legende bei Hroswitha: Bemerkungen zu ihrer literarischen Technik," in *Historische Vierteljahrschrift*, Vol. 30, Dresden, 1935, pp. 168–174, and 361–397.

257. Gertrud Bäumer (1873–1954), *Adelheid Mutter der Königreiche*, Tübingen, 1936.

About the visit of Empress Adelheid (931–999) to Gandersheim, p. 513.

258. Hans Bork, "Hroswitha von Gandersheim," in W. Stammler, ed., *Die deutsche Literatur des Mittelalters: Verfasserlexikon*, Vol. 2, Berlin, 1936, pp. 506–514.

See No. 301.

259. Wolfgang Goetz (1885–), "Hrotsvit rediviva," in *Deutsche Rundschau*, Vol. 246, Berlin, 1936, pp. 89–90.

260. Julian M. Cotton, "La sacra rappresentazione di Lorenzo il Magnifico e il Gallicanus di Rosvita," in *Giornale storico della letteratura Italiana*, Vol. 111, 1938, pp. 77–87.

261. Filippo Ermini, *Medio Evo latino: Studi e ricerche* (Series title: *Studi e testi dell'istituto di filologia romanza dell'Università di Roma*), Modena, 1938.

About Hroswitha, pp. 161–181.

262. Ezio Franceschini (1906–), "Per una revisione del teatro latino di Rosvita," in *Rivista italiana del dramma*, Anno II, Vol. 1, Part 3, Rome, 1938, pp. 300–316.

263. Rudolf Alexander Schröder (1878–), "Roswitha von Gandersheim," in *Niedersachsen*, Vol. 43, Hanover, 1938, pp. 173–179.

264. Rozaliya Iosifovna Shor (1893–1939), *Khrestomatiya po zapadnoevropeisko literatura: Literatura srednikh vekov* (*Anthology of Western European Literature: The Literature of the Middle Ages*), Vol. 1, Moscow, 1938.

Russian translation of *Dulcitius*, Scene 2, pp. 33–35. The author was a Russian philologist.

265. Silvio D'Amico (1887–1955), *Storia del teatro drammatico*, Vol. 1, Milan, 1939.

About Hroswitha, pp. 282–291.

266. *Dictionnaire de théologie catholique*, Vol. 14, Part 1, Paris, 1939.

There is a comprehensive article about Hroswitha by P. Séjourné on pp. 12–16.

111

267. Ezio Franceschini, "I 'tibicines' nella poesia di Hrotsvitha," in *Archivum Latinitatis Medii Aevii*, Vol. 14, Brussels, 1939, pp. 40–65.

268. Eva May Newnan (1892–), *The latinity of the works of Hrotsvit of Gandersheim*, Chicago, 1939 (thesis, Ph.D., University of Chicago, 1936).

Haraszti, *op. cit.*, pp. 157–158 and pp. 170–171, Notes 123–126.

269. Fritz Preissl, *Hrotsvith von Gandersheim und die Entstehung des Mittelalterlichen Heldenbildes* (Series title: *Erlanger Arbeiten zur deutschen Literatur*), Erlangen, 1939 (thesis, Erlangen University, 1939).

Includes a bibliography, pp. 60–61.

270. Rudolf Alexander Schröder, "Roswitha von Gandersheim," in *Die Aufsätze und Reden*, 2 vols., Berlin, 1939, in Vol. 1, pp. 142–155.

271. Paul Lehmann, "Nachrichten von der Sponheimer Bibliothek des Abtes Joh. Trithemius," in *Zeitschrift für Bibliothekswissen und Bibliographie* (in Russian: *Zhurnal bïblïotekoznavstva ta bibliografïi*), Vol. 59, Kiev, 1942, p. 454.

The author was a well-known German bibliographer. Cited in a letter from Dr. Schott of the Cologne Universitäts- und Stadtbibliothek to the Hroswitha Club, April 27, 1959.

272. Ezio Franceschini, *Rosvita di Gandersheimi: Appunti delle lezioni di storia della letteratura latina Medievale*, Milan, 1944.

273. Edwin Herman Zeydel (1893–), "Knowledge of Hrotsvitha's works prior to 1500," in *Modern Language Notes*, Vol. 59, No. 6, Baltimore, June, 1944, pp. 382–385.

The author is an American professor, editor, and translator.

274. Edwin Herman Zeydel, "A note on Hrotsvitha's aversion to synalepha," in *Philological Quarterly*, Vol. 23, No. 4, University of Iowa, Iowa City, October, 1944, pp. 379–381.

275. Sister Mary Xavier Hefner (1907–), *The dramatic technique of Roswitha in Paphnutius as compared with that of Terence* (thesis, M.A., St. Louis University, St. Louis, Mo., 1945, unpublished typescript).

Bibliography, pp. 47–50.

276. Sister Mary Edward Mundell (1908–), *Figurative language in Hrotsvitha's epic Gesta Oddonis* (thesis, M.A., St. Louis University, St. Louis, Mo., 1945, unpublished).

277. Zoltán Haraszti (1892–), "The works of Hroswitha," in *More Books, Bulletin of the Boston Public Library*, Vol. 20, Nos. 3 and 4, Boston, Mass., March and April, 1945, pp. 87–119, and 139–173.

A comprehensive summary of arguments regarding the authenticity of Hroswitha's works, which tends to favor Aschbach's theories. The author is an American librarian, former Keeper of Rare Books, Boston Public Library, Boston, Mass.

Illustrations. Two woodcuts from No. 15: Hroswitha kneeling and offering her book to Otto the Great, and the illustration for *Abraham*; a woodcut portrait of Celtes (1505); and a facsimile of several lines from No. 1.

278. Edwin Herman Zeydel, "On the two minor poems in the Hrosvitha codex," in *Modern Language Notes*, Vol. 60, No. 6, Baltimore, June, 1945, pp. 373–376.

A discussion of the four elegiac distichs (found to be not by Hroswitha) and the *Vision of St. John*, which was by Hroswitha; neither of these appeared in No. 15. Zeydel here makes the first English translation of the *Vision of St. John*.

113

279. Edwin Herman Zeydel, "The reception of Hrosvitha by the German humanists after 1493," in *The Journal of English and Germanic Philology*, Vol. 44, No. 3, University of Illinois, Urbana, Ill., July, 1945, pp. 239–249.

280. Edwin Herman Zeydel, "Were Hrostvitha's dramas performed during his [sic] lifetime?" in *Speculum, a Journal of Mediaeval Studies*, Vol. 20, No. 4, Boston, Mass., October, 1945, pp. 443–456.

281. Edwin Herman Zeydel, "The authenticity of Hrotsvitha's works," in *Modern Language Notes*, Vol. 61, No. 1, Baltimore, January, 1946, pp. 50–55.

A soundly reasoned, logical refutation of No. 277 (Haraszti had implied that there was a possibility that all of Hroswitha's works were a forgery).

282. Edwin Herman Zeydel, "Ego clamor validus," in *Modern Language Notes*, Vol. 61, No. 4, Baltimore, April, 1946, pp. 281–283.

283. Robert Herndon Fife (1871–1958), *Hroswitha of Gandersheim*, New York, 1947. Pamphlet.

This text was prepared by Dr. Fife at the request of, and privately printed for, the Hroswitha Club of New York. It is an erudite study of what could be gathered about Hroswitha's life and her times, with a commentary on her works and a summary of the controversy which had been raging over her authenticity for almost one hundred years. Dr. Fife was inclined to agree with Zeydel that Aschbach's arguments are based on too many assumptions. There is a selected biography on pp. 38–40.

284. Edwin Herman Zeydel, "A chronological Hrotsvitha bibliography through 1700, with annotations," in *The Journal*

of English and Germanic Philology, Vol. 46, No. 3, University of Illinois, Urbana, Ill., July, 1947, pp. 290–294.

285. Mario N. Pavia, "Hrosvitha of Gandersheim," in *Folia*, New York, May, 1948, pp. 41–46.

286. Konrad Weiss (1880–1940), "Hrotsvit von Gandersheim," in *Jahrbuch der Droste-Gesellschaft: Westfällische Blätter für Dichtung und Geistesgeschichte*, Vol. 2, Münster, 1948–1950, pp. 235–251.

287. Karl Petry, *Handbuch zur deutschen Literaturgeschichte . . .*, Vol. 1, Cologne, 1949.

About Hroswitha, pp. 159–163.

288. Hugo Kuhn (1909–), "Hrotswiths von Gandersheim dichterisches Programm," in *Deutsche Vierteljahrschrift für Literaturwissenschaft und Geistesgeschichte*, Vol. 24, Stuttgart, 1950, pp. 181–196.

The author is a German philologist.

289. Rudolf Alexander Schröder, "Roswitha von Gandersheim," in *Gesammelte Werke*, Vol. 2, Berlin, 1952, pp. 770–784.

290. *Enciclopedia Cattolica*, Vol. 10, Florence, 1953.

A comprehensive article about Hroswitha on pp. 1402–1404.

291. E[zio] F[ranceschini], "Rosvita, tutto il teatro, traduzione di C. Cremonesi," review in *Aevum*, Vol. 17, 1953, pp. 95–96.

For Cremonesi's translation see No. 76.

292. S. S. Mokuleskii, ed., *Khrestomatiya po istorii Zapadnoev-ropeiskogo teatra* (*Anthology of the History of Western European Theater*), Vol. 1, Moscow, 1953.

Russian translation of *Abraham*, Scenes 5–7, and *Dulcitius*, Scene 2, on pp. 54–60; translator's name is unknown.

293. Giuseppe Valentini (1901–), "Il teatro e la Latinità di Hrotsvitha per M. Rigobon," review in *Letture*, Milan, 1953, p. 24.

For Rigobon's book see No. 246.

294. August Potthast (1824–1898), ed., *Bibliotheca historica Medii Aevi: Wegweiser durch die Geschichtswerke des Europäischen Mittelalters bis 1500*, 2 vols., revised edition, Graz, Austria, 1954.

Long annotated bibliography on Hroswitha in Vol. 1, p. 622. The first edition of this reference work was published in parts, 1895–1896.

295. Sister Mary Marguerite Butler, R.S.M., "Sapientia" and "Dulcitius" (Play Program), University of Michigan, Lydia Mendelssohn Theatre, January 15, 1955.

Synopsis of each play and a brief preliminary comment by Sister Mary Marguerite Butler.

296. Francis Hamill (1904–), "Some unconventional women before 1800: Printers, booksellers and collectors," in *The Bibliographical Society of America, Papers*, Vol. 44, 4th quarter, New York, 1955.

About Hroswitha, p. [5] (of off-print).

297. Tibor Kardos, *A Magyarországi humanizmus kora* (*Humanism in Hungary*), Budapest, 1955.

Pages *363–365* contain a study of Hroswitha's *Dulcitius*, translated into Hungarian, as it appears in the early XVI-century *Sándor Codex* (see No. 7).

298. Rosemary Sprague (1922–), *Heroes of the White Shield*, New York, 1955.

Historical novel of the X century in Norway, mentioning Hroswitha on pp. 160–162.

299. Rosemary Sprague, "Hroswitha: Tenth-century Margaret Webster," in *The Theatre Annual*, Vol. 13, New York, 1955, pp. 16–31.

300. Wolfgang Stammler (1886–), ed., "Hrotsvit von Gandersheim, Nachtrag," in *Die Deutsche Literatur des Mittelalters: Verfasserlexikon*, edited by K. Langosch, 5 vols., Berlin [1931]–1955; in Vol. 5, 1955, pp. 425–426.

See also No. 258.

301. Kurt Herbert Halbach (1902–), "Epik des Mittelalters," in Wolfgang Stammler, ed., *Deutsche Philologie im Aufriss*, Parts 1–23, 2nd ed., Berlin, Bielefeld, and Munich, 1955–1960, pp. 398–683 (in Pts. 13–14).

About Hroswitha, Pt. 13, pp. 460–465.

302. S. S. Mokuleskii, ed., *Istoriya Zapadnoevropeiskogo teatra* (*History of Western European Theater*), Vol. 1, Moscow, 1956.

About Hroswitha, pp. 13–15.

303. Lewis William Spitz (1895–), *Conrad Celtes, the German Arch-Humanist*, Harvard University Press, 1957.

Numerous references to Hroswitha.

304. Edith Deen, "Roswitha: A religious writer of medieval times," in *Great Women of the Christian Faith*, New York, 1959, pp. 326–327.

305. Sister Mary Marguerite Butler, R.S.M., *Hrotsvitha: The Theatricality of Her Plays*, New York, 1960.

306. Bert Nagel (1907–), "Roswitha von Gandersheim," in *Ruperto-Carola* (Bulletin of the University of Heidelberg), XV, Vol. *33*, June, 1963.

307. Bert Nagel, *Hrotsvit von Gandersheim*, Stuttgart, 1965.

Index

Abbildungen und Lebensbeschreibungen berühmter Gelehrten, 83
Abraham: Argument to, 25–26
manuscripts, 42, 43, 47
performances, 35, 36, 37, 38, 39, 40, 41
printed editions, 57, 68, 71, 72, 73, 74, 75, 76, 77
Acts of the Saints, The, 15–16
Adelaide, 8, 9
Adelheid, Empress, 110
Adelheid Mutter der Konigreiche, 110
Aeda, 4–7, 33
Älteste deutsche Dichterin, Die, 90
Älteste Drama in Deutschland: Die Comödien der Nonne Hrotswitha von Gandersheim, Das, 69
Aevum, 109, 115
Agape, 24, 25
Agius (monk), 7
Agnes, 18, 42
"Albrecht Dürer und Roswitha von Gandersheim," 102
Alcuin, 104
Alderspach 22, *see* Munich, Bayerische Staatsbibliothek Clm 2552
Aldhelmus, 46
Algermissen, 9
Allegemeine deutsche Biographie, 95
Allegemeine Geschichte der Literatur des Mittelalters im Abendlande, 94
Allen, Philip Schuyler, 100
Allgemeine Zeitung, 97
Alpers, Paul, 103

Altfrid, Bishop, 4
"Altungarische Übersetzung des Dulcitius der Hrotsuitha, Die," 97
Altzelle, Cistercian Monastery Ms 03 [Works of Hroswitha], 54
America, 109
American Book Collector, The, 109
American Catholic Quarterly Review, 101
Amsell, E., 36
Anastasius, patron saint of Gandersheim, 7
"Anatole France et le theatre de Hrotsvitha: Une source de Thaïs," 107
Anfaenge, Die, 7
Annalium Hirsaugiensium Tomi II, 81, 82
Annalium Paderbonnensium II Partes, 63
Anthony of Hippo, Saint, 11
Antiquedad de la ciudad e eglesia catedral de Tuy, 81
Antiquitates Gandersheimenses, 63
Antiquitates monasticae, 64
"Anzeige Roswitha und Conrad Celtes," 88
Anzeiger für deutsches Altertum, 103
Apocryphal Gospel of Saint James, 15
Archiv für das Studium der neueren Sprachen und Literaturen, 99
Archivum Latinitatis Medii Aevii, 112

Ascensio, 42
Ascension of our Lord, The, 15
Aschbach, Joseph von, 88, 89, 114
Aschbach controversy, 84
Aschendorffs Sammlung lateinischer und griechischer Klassiker, 74
Aufsätze und Reden, Die, 112
"Aus Münchener Handschriften," 94
Ausgewählte Dichtungen, 75
Ausser-europäischen Dramas und der lateinischen Schauspiele nach Christus bis Ende des X Jahrhunderts, Die, 92
Autenrieth, Dr. Johanna, 56
"Authenticity of Hrosvitha's works, The," 114
Aventinus [in German: Johannes Thurnmaier, Turmair, Thurmayr, or Turmeir], 79

Barack, K. A., 70, 89
Bartsch, Karl Friederich Adolf Konrad, 86, 90
Basilius, 17, 42
Baumer, Gertrud, 110
Bavarian National Library, 43
Bayerische Blätter für das Gymnasialschulwesen, 107
Bebel, Heinrich, 79
Beckmann, Dr. Joseph, 56
Bede, 42
Behrens, Dr. Conrad Berthel, 55
Beiträge zur Literaturgeschichte des Mittelalters und der Renaissance, I: Komödie und Tragödie im Mittelalter, 95

119

"Bekehrung der Buhlerin Thais" (The Conversion of the Courtesan Thais), 38. *See also Paphnutius*

"Bekehrung des Feldherrn Gallican" (The Conversion of General Gallican), 39. *See also Gallicanus*

Bendixen, J., 36, 38, 43, 69, 70, 72

"Benedictinerinnenstift Gandersheim und Hrotsuitha, die Zierde des Benedictinerordens, Das," 94

Benediktinerkloster Klus bei Gandersheim und die Bursfelder Reform, Das, 108

Bergman, Sister Mary Bernardine, 27, 41, 76

Berlin, Preussische Staatsbibliothek Theol. lat. fol. 265, 52–53, *plate 10*

Bertold, Luise [or Berthold], 107

Bibliographical Society of America, The, Papers, 116

Biblioteca universale Rizzoli, 77

Bibliotheca historica Medii Aevi: Wegweiser durch die Geschichtswerke des Europaischen Mittelalters bis 1500, 116

Bibliotheca Latina mediae et infimae aetatis, 82

Bibliotheca Teubneriana, 72, 74

Bibliotheca universalis sive catalogus omnium scriptorum, 80

Bilbasov, Vasilii Aleksyeyevich, 91

Blashfield, Evangeline Wilbour (Mrs. E. H.), 102

Bod-codex, 49

Bodo, Heinrich, 54, 59
  Chronicon, 59
  Proëmium, 61
  Syntagma, 59, 60, 61, 64, 67, 97, 108

Bodo's Syntagma de constructione coenobii Gandesiani und die darin uberlieferten Kaiserurkunden in Gesellschaft für ältere deutsche Geschichtskunde, Neues Archiv, 97

Böhmer, Heinrich, 55

Bonniwell, Rev. Dr. William, 56

Book of Examples, 49

Booklet about the glory of the holy Apostles, 49

Bork, Hans, 110

Börsenblatt für den deutschen Buchhandel, 106

Bosio, G., 74

Brandi, Karl, 104

Brant, Sebastian, 78

Braunschweigische Heimat, 104

Braunschweigisches Magazin, 104

Bresslau, Harry, 97

Brinitzer, Carl, 37

Brodführer, Eduard, 35

Bruno, Archbishop of Cologne, 9

Budapest, Egyetemi Könyvtár (University Library) Codex Hungaricus-Universitatis Budapestinensis 6, *see Sándor Codex*

Burdach, Konrad, 103

Burg, Paul, pseud., 106

"Busse der Maria, Die" (The Repentance of Maria), 38. *See also Abraham*

Busti, Friar Bernardino de, 48, 52

Butler, Sister Mary Marguerite, R.S.M., 19, 23, 27–28, 41, 116, 118

Calimachus: Argument to, 25
  manuscripts, 42, 43
  performances of, 36, 39, 40
  printed editions, 57, 67, 68, 72, 73, 74, 75, 76
  stage directions for, 19

Carmen de Gestis Oddonis, see Gesta Oddonis

Carmen de laudibus virginitatis, 46

Carmen de primordiis et fundatoribus coenobii Gandeshemensis, see Primordia

Carter, Barbara Barclay, 109

Catalogue of Early German and French Woodcuts . . . in the British Museum, 57

Catalogus abbatissarum Gandershemensium, 55

Catalogus codicum bibliothecae universitatis Reg. Scientiarum, 93

Catalogus illustrium virorum, 78

Catholic Encyclopedia, 11

Cave, William, 81

Celtes, Conrad, 11, 43, 84, 100, 113
  discovery of *Munich Codex* by, 3, 49
  1501 edition of *Opera*, 3, 8, 19, 47, 52–53, 57, 75
  forgery by, 90
  notes of, 69
  quoted, 50
  reference to, 79

Chaney, William A., 40

Chasles, Victor Euphémion Philarète, 85

Chilianus, Eques Mellerstatinus, 79

Chionia, 24

Christian Iconography, 85

Christine, Abbess of Gandersheim, 8

Chronicon Coenobii Clusini, 59

Chronicon insigne monasterii Hirsaugiensis, 80

"Chronological Hrotsvitha bibliography through 1700, with annotations, A," 58, 114

Chroust, A., 44

"Chute et conversion de Marie, nièce de l'ermite Abraham," 74

"Clamor Validus Gandersheimensis," 11

Classical Journal, 106

Cloak, F. Theodore, 40

Cloetta, Wilhelm, 95

Codex Hungaricus-Universitatis Budapestinensis 6, see Sándor Codex

Coffman, George Raleigh, 103

Cohn, Albert, 87

[Collected plays] (Cremonesi), 77

[Collected plays] (Endepols), 76

Cologne, Historisches Archiv W 101 1, 43–44, *plate 3*

Colophon, The, 108

Comedia gloriose parthenices et martiris Dorothee agoniam passionemque depingens, 79

Commedia Latina del secolo X e una sacra rappresentazione del secolo XV, Una, 93

Commedie, 72

Commedie Latine, Le, 74

Comoedias sex, 43, 69

"Coniectanae," 92

Conigliani, Emma Boghen, 97
Conrad, King of Germany, 8
Conrad Celtes, the German Arch-Humanist, 117
Constance, Princess, 24
Contzen, H. Th., 85
Cornides-codex, 49
Corona della beatissima Vergine Maria, 49
Cotton, Julian M., 111
Coulter, Cornelia Catlin, 106
Cours de littérature Française, 84
Craig, Edith, 36
Creizenach, Wilhelm Michael Anton, 96
Cremonesi, C., 77
Critica spicciola, 94
Cultura Medievale, 74
Cultura, La: Rivista mensile di filosofia, lettere, arte, 105
Curiosités dramatiques et littéraires, 86
Cuspinianus, Johannes [in German: Spiesshaymer], 80
Cuzin, J., 73

Dale, Darley, pseud. [Francesca Maria Steele], 101
D'Amico, Silvio, 74, 111
De Caesaribus atque imperatoribus Romanis opus insigne, 80
De conversione Saxonum, 46
De dictus factisque memorabilibus collectanea, 79
De fundatione coenobii Gandesiani, 60
De Gestis Ottonum, 60, 61
De historicis Latinis libri tres, 81
De Hrosuitha poetria scripsit et comoediam Abraham inscriptam adjecit, 85
De scriptoribus ecclesiasticis, 78
De vita et scriptis Conradi Celtis protucii, 84
Deen, Edith, 118
Desirio, Eugene, 40
Deutsche Dichter des lateinischen Mittelalters in deutschen Versen, 72
"Deutsche Dichtung im lateinischen Gewande: Eine Problembetrachtung," 110
Deutsche Dichtungen des lateinischen Mittelalters für den deutsch- und latein Unterricht, 74

Deutsche Heimat Blätter für Literatur und Volkstum, 98
Deutsche Kultur- und Sittengeschichte, 86
Deutsche Literatur des Mittelalters: Verfasserlexikon, Die, 110, 117
Deutsche Literaturzeitung, 107
Deutsche Philologie im Aufriss, 117
Deutsche Rundschau, 104, 110
Deutsche Vierteljahrschrift für Literaturwissenschaft und Geistesgeschichte, 103, 115
Deutschlands Geschichtsquellen im Mittelalter bis zur Mitte des dreizehnten Jahrhunderts, 87
Dictionnaire de théologie catholique, 111
"Did Hrotswitha imitate Terence?," 98
Didron, Adolphe Napoléon, 85–86
Diocletian, 24, 48
Dionysius, 42
Dionysius of Athens, 17
Distichon Distrophon, 62
Dodgson, Campbell, 57
"Doigt de Dieu, Le," 39. *See also Calimachus*
Dolenz, S., 74
Donahue, Tom, 40
Dorer-Egloff, Ignatius Eduard, 86
Drake, William A., 102
Drama of the Medieval Church, The, 109
Dramatic technique of Roswitha in Paphnutius as compared with that of Terence, The, 113
Dramen, Die, 71, 73, 76
Drammi mistici, 74
"Drei Beiträge zur Roswitha-Forschung: Zum 1,000 Geburtstag der ersten deutschen Dichterin," 109
Drusiana, 25
Du Méril, Édélstand Pontas, 85
Dublin Review, The, 109
Dürer, Albrecht, 8, 57
Dulcitius: Argument to, 24–25
manuscripts, 42, 43, 47–49, 57
performances of, 35, 36, 37–38, 40, 41

printed editions, 57, 67, 68, 70, 72, 75, 76, 77
references to, 87–88, 90, 93, 117

Eberhard, Duke of the Franks, 8
Eberhard, priest, 11
Ebert, Adolf, 94
Ebert, Councillor, 54
Eckenstein, Lina, 96
Edith of England, 8
"Ego clamor validus," 114
"Ehrenrettung des Ligurinus, Die," 91
Enciclopedia Cattolica, 115
Endepols, J. H. E., 76
Endlicher, Stephen Ladislaus, 84
English Historical Review, 95
Enter the Actress, the First Women in the Theatre, 107
"Epik des Mittelalters," 117
Epistola ad Ioannem Nauclerum alias Fergenhans, qui auctores legendi sint novitiis ad comparandam eloquentiam, 79
Erlanger Arbeiten zur deutschen Literatur, 112
Ermini, Filippo, 72, 73, 105, 106, 111
Erwachung des Calimachus: Ein Schauspiel, Die, 73
"Erweckung des Calimachus, Die," 36. *See also Calimachus*
Esprit des journeaux, François et étrangers, 83
Étude sur l'Allemagne ancienne et moderne, 85
Études sur les premiers temps du Christianisme et sur le Moyen Age, 85
Euringer, Sebastian, 109
European and Asiatic Plays, 75

Fabius, 48
Fabricius, Johann Albert, 82
"Fall und Busse der Maria" (The Fall and Repentance of Maria), 38. *See also Abraham*
Fall and Conversion of Theophilus, The, 16–17
story, 16–17
Fanfulla della Domenica, 94
Festgabe für H. Gauert, 100

121

Festschrift zur Vierhundert-jahrfeier des Alten Gymnasiums zu Bremen, 74
Fiera letteraria, 106
Fife, Robert Herndon, 12, 114
Figurative language in Hrotsvitha's epic Gesta Oddonis, 113
Film and Theatre Today, 76
Fischer, Ivo, 105
Fliegel, Alice, 38
Folia, 115
Forschungen zur deutschen Geschichte, 90, 91
Forsythe, Robert Stanley, 110
Fr. Henrici Bodonis Syntagma de Ecclesia Gandesiana ex MSto emendatum atque supplementum, 62
France, Anatole, pseud. [Jacques Anatole Franc Thibault], 35, 95
Franceschini, Ezio, 111, 112, 115
Franz, Lothar, 46
Fregoso, Battista [in Latin: Fulgosius], 79
Frenken, Goswin, 44, 102, 107
Freytag, Gustav, 85
Fries, Ellen, 95

"Gallicano di Rosvita e il Martirio dei Sancti Giovanni e Paolo di Lorenzo il Magnifico, Il," 93
Gallicanus: Argument to, 23–24
  manuscripts, 42, 43, 45
  performances of, 39, 40
  printed editions, 57, 67, 75, 76
  references to, 90
  stage directions for, 19
"Gallicanus di Rosvita e il San Giovanni e Paolo di Lorenzo il Magnifico, Il," 93
Gandersheim Abbey, *ill.*, 10
Gandersheim Cloister Church, *ill.*, 32
Gandersheim, Map of old, *ill.*, 66
Gartenlaube, 102
Gasquet, Cardinal, 3
Geistliche Spiele: Lateinische Dramen des Mittelalters mit deutschen Versen, 77
Gerberga I, 8

Gerberga II, Princess, 4, 8, 9, 14, 22, 28, 34, 43
  dedications to, 13, 15, 17, 29–30
Germania, 86, 90
Gesammelte Werke, 115
Gesamtkatalog der Wiegendrucke, 79
Geschichte der Bildung Beraubung und Vernichtung der alten heidelbergischen Büchersammlungen, 83
Geschichte der deutschen Literatur des 11. und 12. Jahrhunderts, 92
Geschichte der lateinischen Literatur des Mittelalters, 100
Geschichte der Roswitha, eines Stiftsfräuleins von Gandersheim, 82
Geschichte der ungarischen Literatur im Mittelalter, 87
Geschichte des Dramas, 92
Geschichte des neueren Dramas, Vol. I: Mittelalter und Frührenaissance, 96
Geschichte Oddos des Grossen, 69
Geschichtsschreiber der deutschen Vorzeit, X Jahrhundert, Die, 70
Geschichtsschreiber der sächsischen Kaiserzeit, 85
Gesellschaft für ältere deutsche Geschichtskunde, Neues Archiv, 94, 101, 102
Gesner, Conrad von, 80
Gesta Oddonis, 8, 27–33
  manuscripts, 42, 46, 52–53
  printed editions, 58, 59, 63, 64, 68, 69, 70, 71, 75, 76
  quoted, 28–29
Ghilini, Camillo, 79
Gichtel, Dr. H. I. A., 56
Giehlow, Dr. Karl, 57
Gilder, Rosamond, 106, 107
Giornale Napoletano de filosofia e lettere, 93
Giornale storico della letteratura Italiana, 111
Giraldi, Lilio Gregorio [in Latin: Gyraldus, Lilius Gregorius], 80
Gödeke, Karl Friederick Ludwig, 93
Goetting, 7, 9
Göttingische Gelehrte Anzeigen, 89

Goetz, Wolfgang, 110
Gongolf, 15
"Gongolf-Legende bei Hroswitha: Bemerkungen zu ihrer literarischen Technik, Die," 110
Gongolfus, 42, 71
Gottsched, Johann Christoph, 67
Gourmont, Rémy de, 100
Gout, Raoul, 107
Grashof, Otto, 94
Great Women of the Christian Faith, 118
Gresemund, Theodore, Jr., 46
Groesbeck, Amy, 39
Grundrisz zur Geschichte der deutschen Dichtung aus den Quellen, Vol. 1: Das Mittelalter, 93
Guignard, Jacques, 39
Gundlach, Wilhelm, 71

Hadrian, 26–27
Halbach, Kurt Herbert, 117
Hamberger, Georg Christoph, 83
Hamill, Francis, 116
Handbuch der Altertumswissenschaft, 100
Handbuch zur deutschen Literaturgeschichte, 115
Handschriften der Herzoglichen Bibliothek zu Wolfenbüttel: Zweite Abteilung, Die Augusteischen Handschriften IV, Die, 97
Handschriftenverzeichnis der Kärtner Bibliotheken, 105
Handschriftenverzeichnisse der Königlichen Bibliothek zu Berlin, 99
Handschriftenverzeichnisse Österreichischer Bibliotheken, 105
Hanover, former Royal Library, Case No. VI (Bibl. Meibom No. 64), 56
Hanover Royal Public Library, Ms XXIII: 548, 60
Haraszti, Zoltán, 56, 57, 113
Harenberg, Johann Christoph, 67
Harms, C., 74
Harrsen, Meta, 49
Hart, J. M., 98
Hartfelder, Karl, 93

Harz: Monatsschrift des Harz-
klubs, 106
Hathmodo, Abbess of Gan-
dersheim, 7
Haupt, Moritz, 92
Hauser, George, 40
Hayley, William, 67, 83
Heard, John, 75, 110
Hedwig, 9
Hefner, Sister Mary Xavier,
41, 113
Heidelberg, Universitäts-
bibliothek Cod. Pal. Germ.
298, 47, plate 8
"Heilige und die Dirne: Eine
Motivgeschichtliche Studie
zu Hrotsvits Abraham und
Paphnutius, Der," 107
"Heimkehr einer Verirrten"
(The Return of the Confused
One), 37. See also Abraham
Heinemann, Otto von, 59, 97
Heinrich, Guillaume Alfred, 91
Heinrici Bodonis chronici
Gandeshemensis supplementum
ex MSto, 62
Heldenlieder der deutschen
Kaiserzeit . . . Erster Band, 71
Hell, Theodor, pseud. [Carl
Gottfried Theodor Winkler],
84
Henry, Duke of Bavaria, 8,
28, 43
Henry the Fowler, 8, 20, 27
Herbst, Hermann, 108
Hermes: Zeitschrift für klas-
sische Philologie, 92
Heroes of the White Shield, 117
Herold, A.-Ferdinand, 71
Herzog August Bibliothek,
Wolfenbüttel, 54, 59, 61
Hildesheim Chronical, 27–28
Hirsch, F., 98
Histoire de la littérature Alle-
mande, 91
Historia ecclesiae Ganders-
hemensis . . . in supplementum
. . . scriptorum rerum Bruns-
vicensium Leibnizianae
adornatum, 67
Historia poetarum et poematum
medii aevi decem, . . . Halae
Magdeb [urgicae], 82
Historiae poetarum . . . dialogi
decem, quibus scripta et vitae
eorum sic exprimuntur, 80
Historische Gesellschaft: Mit-

teilungen aus der historischen
Literatur, 98
Historische Studien, 84
Historische Vierteljahrschrift,
110
Historische Zeitschrift, 91
Historischen Vereins von Ober-
pfalz und Regensburg, Ver-
handlungen, 92
Historischer Verein von Unter-
franken und Aschaffenburg,
Archiv, 105
Historisches Jahrbuch der
Görresgesellschaft, 109
Hoch- und wohlgelehrte deutsche
Frauenzimmer, Das, 82
Hörmann, Dr. W., 56
Hoffman, Susanne, 104
Holder-Egger, O., 45, 94
Holtgot, Robertus, 44–45
Holthusen, Dr. Marc, 59, 62
Homerus Latinus, 43
Homeyer, Helene, 75
Horvath, János, 107
"Hrosvita, de la comédie au
dixième siècle: Paphnuce et
Thaïs," 68
"Hrosvita: Naissance du
drame chrétien au Xe siècle,"
85
"Hrosvitha . . . die älteste
deutsche Dichterin," 93
"Hrosvitha of Gandersheim"
(Hudson), 95
"Hrosvitha of Gandersheim"
(Pavia), 115
"Hrosvitha's Ottolied über-
setzt . . . von W. Gundlach,"
96
"Hrosvits literarische Stel-
lung," 99
Hroswitha I, 8, 11
"Hroswitha" (Conigliani), 97
"Hroswitha" (Panzacchi), 94
"Hroswitha aux marion-
nettes," 95
Hroswitha-Gedenkfeier im Tausendjährigen Gandersheim, 74
Hroswitha of Gandersheim:
Arguments to the plays,
23–27
education, 12
historical epics, 27–34
life, 4
poetical form, 13
prefaces, 13–15, 20–21, 22–
23, 29–30, 31–33

rhymed dramas, 19–22
sacred legends, 15–19
sources, 18–19
works, 3
Hroswitha of Gandersheim
(Fife), 114
"Hroswitha: Tenth-century
Margaret Webster," 117
"Hroswitha von Ganders-
heim" (Bork), 110
Hroswithae liber tertius, 76
"Hroswitha's abbey," 108
Hrotsuit von Gandersheim
(Köpke), 67, 90
Hrotsuit von Gandersheim
(Walderdorff), 92
Hrotsuitha, Gandersheim, and
the Saxon house, 104
Hrotsuitha Gedicht über Gan-
dersheims Gründung und die
Thaten Kaiser Oddo I, Der,
70
Hrotsuithas Frauen-Gestalten,
99
"Hrotsvit rediviva," 110
"Hrotsvit von Ganders-
heidiem, erste niedersächsi-
sche Dichterin," 103
"Hrotsvit von Gandersheim"
(Brandi), 104
Hrotsvit von Gandersheim
(Nagel), 35, 118
"Hrotsvit von Gandersheim"
(Ostheide), 98
"Hrotsvit von Gandersheim"
(Strecker), 99
"Hrotsvit von Gandersheim"
(Weiss), 115
"Hrotsvit von Gandersheim,
Nachtrag," 117
Hrotsvith von Gandersheim und
die Entstehung des Mittel-
alterlichen Heldenbildes, 112
"Hrotsvitha en Waltharius,"
100
"Hrotsvitha, the nun of
Gandersheim, A.D. 930?
935?–1005?," 110
"Hrotsvitha, the strong voice
of Gandersheim," 106
"Hrotsvitha, a tenth-century
nun—The first woman play-
wright," 107
Hrotsvitha: The Theatricality of
Her Plays, 118
"Hrotsvitha und ihre Zeit," 87
Hrotsvithae Opera, 27

"Hrotsvithae opera, recensuit et emendavit Paul de Winterfeld," 98

"Hrotsvithae opera, recensuit et emendavit Paulus de Winterfeld," 98

Hrotsvitha's Ottolied, 71

"Hrotsviths Charakter," 107–108

"Hrotsvits literarische Stellung," 72

Hrotsvits Maria und Pseudo-Matthaeus, 98

Hrotswith and Terence, 99

"Hrotswitha the poetess of Gandersheim," 103

"Hrotswiths von Gandersheim dichterisches Programm,"115

Hudson, William Henry, 95

Humour in Varro and Other Essays, 106

"Humour of Hrotsvitha, a medieval nun, The," 106

Illustrierte Zeitung, 105

Imperatoris Henrici Quarti vita: Epistola ad Ambrosium, 79

Incunabula in American Libraries. A Second Census, 78

Innocent, patron saint of Gandersheim, 7

Irena, 24

Irodalmi müveltségunk kezdetei (The Origins of our Literary Education), 107

Istoriya srednickh vekov v yeie sisatelyakh i issledovaniyakh noveishikh uchenykh (History of the Middle Ages, as Represented in the Period's Writers and Latest Scientists' Research), 101

Istoriya Zapadnoevropeiskogo teatra (History of Western European Theater), 117

Jahrbuch der Droste-Gesellschaft: Westfällische Blätter für Dichtung und Geistesgeschichte, 115

Jahrbücher der Literatur, 84

Jarcho, Boris Isaakovich [in Russian: Yarkho], 103–104, 105

John, Grand Almoner to Constance, 24

John the Apostle, St., 25

John the Bishop, 15

John XII, Pope, 8

Journal of English and Germanic Philology, The, 58, 114, 115

Julian the Apostate, 24

Kaeppeli, Dr. Thomas, 45

Kaiserlichen Akademie der Wissenschaften Wien, Philosophisch-historische Klasse, Sitzungsberichte, 88

Kanonissenstifte, 7

Kardos, Tibor, 50, 116

Katalog der Handschriften der Universitätsbibliothek in Heidelberg, Vol 2: Die deutschen Pfalzer Handschriften des 16. und 17. Jahrhunderts, 98

Katona, L., 48, 49, 51, 97

Kemp-Welch, Alice (Mrs. W.), 99, 101

Kent, W. H., 74

Khrestomatiya po istorii Zapadnoevropeiskogo teatra (Anthology of the History of Western European Theater), 116

Khrestomatiya po zapadnoevropeisko literatura: Literatura srednikh vekov (Anthology of Western European Literature: The Literature of the Middle Ages), 111

Kirpichnikov, Aleksandr Ivanovich, 89, 90

Klagenfurt, Austria, Studienbibliothek Ms 44, 44–45, plate 4

Klagenfurt 52, 44–45

Klein, Julius Leopold, 92

Klimberg, J., 74

Klüpfel, Engelbert, 84

"Knowledge of Hrotsvitha's works prior to 1500," 112

Knuth, Gustav, 37

Köpke, Ernst Rudolf Anastasius, 67, 80, 88, 90

Kolbenheyer, Moritz, 87

Koniklijke Vlaamsche Academie vor Taal-en Letterkunde, Verslagen en Mededeelingen, 100

Kreemers, Ralph, 106

Kriesblatt, 38

Kronenberg, Kurt, 11

Kublitskii, Mikhail, 87

Kuehne, Oswald Robert, 102, 103

Kuhn, Hugo, 115

Kuttnig, Dr., 56

la Bretonne, Vignon Rétif de, 69

Lambert, Agnes L., 73

Lambert, R. S., 73

Langosch, Karl, 77

Lateinische und griechische Lesehefte, 75

Lateinische Reimprosa, Die, 104

Latin mystique, Le, 100

Latinity of the works of Hrotsvit of Gandersheim, The, 112

Lawren, Joseph, 36

Leesdrama's, 76

"Legenden der h. Agape, Ciona, und Irene," 88

Lehmann, Paul, 100, 112

Lehmann-Haupt, Hellmut, 104

Leibniz, Gottfried Wilhelm von, 55, 59, 61, 62, 63, 64, 67, 82

Leipziger Studien aus dem Gebiet der Geschichte, 55

Lettere e arti, 95

Letture, 116

Leuckfeld, Johann Georg, 55, 63–64, 67

Leyser, Polycarp, 82

Lieftinck, Dr. G. I., 56

Literarisches Centralblatt für Deutschland, 98

Literary Women of England, The, 87

Literaturnaya mozaika (Literary Mosaic), 87

Liudolf, Duke of Swabia, 4–7, 27, 33, 55

Liudolf, Prince, 28

Löher, Franz von, 87

Lone, E[mma] Miriam, 108, 109

Loparco, L., 93

Lothar II, 8

"Loud cry of Gandersheim, The," 109

Louis (Ludovic the German), 7

Lucas, Hippolyte Julien Joseph, 86

Lübeck, Georg-Philip Schmidt, von, 84

M. . . . s, M., 98
Maas, Gerhard, 38
Mabillon, J., 82
McAdoo, Eva, 39
McCann, A. F., 72
Machaut, Guillaume de, 41
McIntyre, Andrina, 38
Märkvärdiga qvinnor: Ut-
  ländka qvinnor (Remarkable
  Women: Foreign Women), 95
Magnin, Charles, 68, 85
Magyarországi humanizmus
  kora, A (Humanism in
  Hungary), 116
Mainz, Willigis von, 55
Manitius, Maximilianus, 100
Manuel de bibliographie biogra-
  phique et d'iconographie des
  femmes célèbres, 96
Maria: description, 15
  manuscripts, 42, 44–45
Marionnettes de M. Signoret,
  Les," 95
Mary, niece of Abraham, 25–
  26
Matilda, 20
Mattrai, L., 49
Maugérard, Jean-Baptiste, 83
Mayer, Anton, 107
"Mediaeval mimus, Part II,
  The," 100
Medieval Library, The, 73
Medio Evo latino: Studi e
  ricerche, 111
Meibom, Heinrich (the elder),
  58, 63, 69
Meibom, Heinrich [or May-
  baum] (the younger), 54,
  58–59, 69
  Gesta Oddonis, 64
  Proëmium, 62
  Scriptores, 62
  Syntagma, 60
Menhardt, Hermann, 44, 45,
  104, 105
Mercure de France, 107
Meyensis, Frater Valerius, 52
Migne, J.-P., 69
"Millénaire de Hrotsvitha,
  Le," 74
Millington, E. J., 85
"Mimus," 100
Mistici, 74
Mitteilungen des Instituts für
  Österreichische Geschichte, 96
Modern Language Notes, 98,
  112, 113, 114

Modern Philology, 100, 103
Mokuleskii, S. S., 116, 117
"Monaca e romanziere," 95
"Monakhinya Rosvita: Iz
  poemy ob Ottone Velikkom,
  949–952" ("The Nun
  Hroswitha: From the poem
  about Otto the Great, 949–
  952"), 101
"Monakhina Rosvita, pisatel'-
  nitza X viecka" ("The nun
  Hroswitha, writer of the
  tenth century"), 91
Monasterii Veteris Cellae
  abbates, 54
Monck, Nugent, 36
Monumenta Christiana, 76
Monumenta Germaniae Histo-
  rica, Scriptorum, 55, 56, 68
More Books, Bulletin of the
  Boston Public Library, 56,
  57, 113
Morti e vivanti, 97
Mosa, Leonide, 40
Mundell, Sister Mary Edward,
  113
Munich, Bayerische Staats-
  bibliothek Clm 14485, 42–43,
  plates 1, 2. See also Munich
  Codex
Munich, Bayerische Staats-
  bibliothek Clm 2552, 45–46,
  plate 5
Munich Codex, 3, 19

"Nachlass des Abtes Tri-
  themius von St. Jakob in
  Würzburg, Der," 105
"Nachrichten von der Spon-
  heimer Bibliothek des Abtes
  Joh. Tritheimius," 100, 112
Nagel, Bert, 35, 41, 118
Nelidoff, Wladimir, 36
"Neue Hrotsvithhandschrift,
  Eine," 102
Neue Jahrbücher für das klas-
  sische Altertum Geschichte
  und deutsche Literatur, und für
  Pädegogik, 99
Neue Jahrbücher für Wissen-
  schaft und Jugendbildung, 110
Neumann, Friedrich, 37
"New approach to Medieval
  Latin drama, A," 103
New York Post, 39
Newnan, Eva May, 112
Niedersachsen, 103, 111

Nineteenth Century and After,
  The, 99
Nobbe, K. F. A., 69
Nöthiger Vorrath zur Ge-
  schichte der deutschen drama-
  tischen Dichtkunst, 67
Nomina Abbatissarum Ecclesiae
  Gandesianae in ordinem, quo
  praefuerunt, redacta, 62
Nomina Episcopum Hildesia-
  norum et ordo eorundem, 62
Non-dramatic works of
  Hroswitha, The, 76
Norden, Fritz, 74
"Note on Hrotsvitha's aver-
  sion to synalepha, A," 113
Notes and Queries for Readers
  and Writers, Collectors and
  Librarians, 110
"Notice de l'édition originale
  des oeuvres de Hrotsvite,
  dont il existe un magnifique
  exemplaire dans la biblio-
  thèque de Mgr. l'archevêque
  de Toulouse," 83
"Notice sur le théâtre de
  Hrotswitha," 91
"Nun Hroswitha and her
  writings, The," 96
Nuova antologia, 105
Nyelvemlékeink a könyvyomtatás
  koráig (Our Linguistic Records Up to the Age of
  Printing), 96
Nyelvemléktár regi Magyar
  codexek és nyomtatvanyok
  (Collection of Linguistic Relics
  of Ancient Hungarian Mss
  and Printed Books), 70

Obermeier, Sister M. Hilda,
  104
Ocherki iz istorii srednevekovot
  literatury (Essays in the
  History of Medieval Litera-
  ture), 89
Oda, 4–7, 33
Oeuvres complètes, 95
Oeuvres dramatiques, 72
Of Six Mediaeval Women, 101
"On the two minor poems in
  the Hrosvitha codex," 113
Opera (Celtes), 57, 85–86
Opera (Migne), 69
Opera (Schurtzfleisch), 63
Opera (Strecker), 72, 74
Opera (Winterfeld), 71

"Opere di Hrosvitha, Le," 105
Opera Historica, . . ., 81
"Opera Hrosvite illustris
monialis," 54
*Operum tomi quarti pars
secunda continens opuscula ad
historiam et antiquitates per-
tinentia,* 82
"Original-codex der Roswitha
und die Herausgabe des-
selben durch Conrad Celtes,
Der," 86
*Origines Latines du théâtre
moderne, Les,* 85
O'Shea, M., 39
Osservatore Romano, 37
Ostheide, Albert, 98
Ottenthal, Emil von, 96
Otto I (the Great), 8, 9, 22,
108
dedication to, 31
in *Gesta Ottonis,* 27, 28
Otto II, 9, 22, 34
dedication to, 31–33
in *Gesta Ottonis,* 27, 28
Otto III, 9, 34
Otto the Illustrious, 7, 34
*Ottonian Dynasty, The,
facing page* 8
*Ottonische Studien zur deutschen
Geschichte im zehnten Jahr-
hundert,* 67, 88, 90
Oudin, [Remi] Casmiro, 81

*Pafnutius, see Paphnutius
Panegyric Oddonum, see Gesta
Oddonis*
Pannenborg, A., 91
Panzacchi, Enrico, 94, 95, 97
Paphnutius: Argument to, 26
manuscript, 42
performances of, 35, 36, 37,
38, 39, 40
printed editions, 57, 68, 71,
72
Patrologiae cursus completus, 69
Paul, Grand Almoner to
Constance, 24
Paul, Saint, 16, 17
Paullini, Franz Christian, 82
Pavia, Mario N., 115
Pelagius, 42
story of, 16, 18
Penelope für 1821, 84
"Per una revisione del teatro
latino di Rosvita," 111
Perk, Marie Adrien, 94

Pertz, G. H., 54, 56, 68, 71
Petit, Élie, 89, 90
Petry, Karl, 115
Pfund, T. G. M., 70
Philological Quarterly, 113
*Philosophical, Historical and
Moral Essay on Old Maids,
A,* 67, 83
Pighi, B. G., 109
Piltz, O., 41, 71, 73, 76
Plays of Hroswitha, The
(St. John), 20–21, 73
Plays of Roswitha, The (Till-
yard), 36, 73
"Poèmes latins de Hrotswitha,
Les," 90
Poemetti di Hrotsvit, I, 73
Poésies Latines, 69
Poet Lore, 75, 110
Poeti epici Latini del secolo X,
73
Pogodin, Aleksandr L'vovich,
101
Polcheim, K., 104
Pommersfelden Castle, Upper
Franconia, Library of Count
Schoenborn Ms 308 (2883),
46, *plates 6, 7*
Portraits and Backgrounds, 102
Potthast, August, 116
Praefatiuncula, 54, 59, 60,
61, 62
*Praelectiones in librum sapien-
tiae,* 45
Preissl, Fritz, 76, 112
*Primi et antiquissimi Saxonicae
scriptoris Witichindi. . . anna-
lium libri tres,* 58
Primordia: Allied to *Gesta
Ottonis,* 27, 42, 54
history of Gandersheim, 4–7
manuscript, lost, 54–56
printed editions, 63, 64, 67,
68, 69, 70, 75, 76
title page of, *ill.,* 65
writing of, 33–34
*Primordia Coenobii
Gandeshemensis, see Primordia
Proëmium,* 60, 61, 62

"Quadrivium in den Dichtun-
gen Roswithas von Ganders-
heim, Das," 100
"Quadrivium in Dichtungen
Roswithas, von P.A. Sturm,
Das," 101

*R. Università di Padova. Pub-
licazioni della facoltà di lettere
e filosofia,* 108
Rattenbury, Arnold, 76
Raynal, Raymond, 39
"Reception of Hrosvitha by the
German humanists after 1493,
The," 114
Reclams Universal-Bibliothek, 76
Reich, H., 72
Reinicke, F., 106
Rerum Germanicarum Tomi III,
58
Reubelt, Frances, 99
Reuber, Justus, 58, 64,
*Revelation of St. John, see Vision
of St. John*
Revue d'Allemagne, 74
Revue de l'art Chrétien, 89, 90
Revue des deux mondes, 68, 85
"Rezension der Streckerschen
Hrotswith-Ausgabe," 107
Rigobon, Marcella, 108
Rikkardis, 14
Rivista italiana del dramma,
111
Roberts, Arthur J., 98
Roennecke, Dr., 37
Röse, Friedrich, 105
Roethe, Gustav, 102
Romanus II, 9
*Rosarium sermonum per totum
annum,* 48
Rose, Valentin, 99
Rosenfeld, Sybil, 41
Rosenthal, J., 55
Rostrup, Dr. Egil, 39
*Rosvita di Gandersheimi: Ap-
punti delle lezioni di storia della
letteratura latina Medievale,*
112
"Rosvita" (Tecchi), 106
"Rosvita" (Vignola), 105
"Rosvita, tutto il teatro, tradu-
zione di C. Cremonesi," 115
"Roswitha" (Allen), 100
"Roswitha: Biographische
Skizze," 84
*Roswitha, die nonne von Ganders-
heim,* 86
"Roswitha, een toneelsch-
rijfster von 1,000 jaar terug,"
106
"Roswitha, nun and dramatist,"
101
"Roswitha of Gandersheim"
(Carter), 109

"Roswitha of Gandersheim" (Drake), 102
"Roswitha: A religious writer of medieval times," 118
"Roswitha-Tag in Gandersheim," 106
Roswitha und Conrad Celtes, 88, 89
"Roswitha und Conrad Celtes von Joseph Aschbach," 89
"Roswitha von Gandersheim" (Nagel), 118
"Roswitha von Gandersheim" (Schmid), 95
"Roswitha von Gandersheim" (Schröder), 111, 112, 115
Roswitha von Gandersheim, die erste deutsche Dichterin, 100
"Roswitha von Gandersheim: Zur tausendsten Wiederkehr des Geburtstages der ersten deutschen Dichterin," 106
Ruberto, L., 93
Rüde, Bernd, 41
Ruef, J. C., 84
Ruland, Anton, 86, 89
Ruperto-Carola, 118

"Sacra rappresentazione di Lorenzo il Magnifico e il Gallicanus di Rosvita, La," 111
Saggi Critici, 94
St. John, Christopher, pseud. [Christabel Marshall], 20, 27, 36, 38, 39, 73
St. Emmeram, Regensburg, E. CVIII, *see* Munich, Bayerische Staatsbibliothek Clm 14485
Samtliche Werke herausgegeben von der Kgl. senschaften, 79–80
Sándor, István, 48
Sándor Codex, 47–52, 70, 87–88, 93, 96, 107, 117, *plate 9*
Sandoval, Prudencio de, 81
Sands, Dorothy, 39
Sapientia: Argument to, 26–27
   manuscripts, 42, 44–45
   performances of, 40, 41
   printed editions, 57, 76
Schaten, Nicolaus, 55, 63
Schaumburg, Paul Erich Bruno Richard, 106
Scheffer, Mrs. Nathalie, 91
Scherer, Wilhelm, 92
Scherr, Johannes, 86
Schmid, Otto, 95

Schneiderhan, Johann, 100
Scholz, János, 49, 107
Schott, Dr., 112
Schröckh, Johann Matthias, 83
Schroeder, Edward, 103
Schröder, Rudolf Alexander, 111, 112, 115
Schulhoff, Else, 36, 38, 39, 73
Schulte, J., 74
Schurtzfleisch, H. L., 63, 69
Scriptores rerum Brunsvicensium illustrationi inservientes, 62, 64
Scriptores rerum Germanicarum in usum scholarum ex monumentis Germaniae historicis, 71
Scriptorum, 68
Scriptorum ecclesiasticorum historia literaria a Christo nato usque ad saeculum, XIV; XV, 81
Séjourné, P., 111
Selected works (*Theophilus, Dulcitius, Gesta Oddonis*, and *Primordia Gandeshemensis*, 75
Serapeum, Zeitschrift für Bibliothekwissenschaft, Handschriftenkunde und ältere Literatur, 86, 88
Sergius II, Pope, 7
Shakespeare in Germany in the Sixteenth and Seventeenth Centuries, 87
Shor, Rozaliya Iosifovna, 111
"Short sketch of the life and works of Hroswitha, the nun-poetess, A," 109
Signoret, M., 35
Simons, Dr. L., 100
Sisinnius, 24, 48
Slater, Montague, 76
"Some bookwomen of the fifteenth century," 108
"Some unconventional women before 1800: Printers, book-sellers and collectors," 116
Sommer, P. K., 102
Sophia, Abbess of Gandersheim, 34
Sorbelli, T., 74
Speculum, a Journal of Mediaeval Studies, 105, 114
Spitz, Lewis William, 117
Spörri, Reinhart, 40
Sprague, Rosemary, 117
Stach, Walter, 110
Stahl, Leopold, 37

Stammler, Wolfgang, 117
Stasyulebich, Mikhail Matveyevich, 101
Steele, Francesca Maria, 101
Steinhoff, R., 93
Stillwell, Margaret B., 78
"Stilquellen der Hrotsvitha," 103
Storia del teatro drammatico, 111
Strecker, Karl, 27, 72, 74, 98, 99, 101, 107
Strunk, J. E., 63
Studi letterari, 97
Studi Medievali, 106
Studi e testi dell'istituto di filologia romanza dell'Università di Roma, 111
Studien und Mitteilungen aus dem Benedictiner- und dem Cistercienser-Orden, 94
Studien und Mitteilungen zur Geschichte des Benediktiner-Ordens und seiner Zeit, 100
Study of the Thaïs legend, with special reference to Hroswitha's Paphnutius, A, 102
"Study of the Thaïs legend with special reference to Hrosvitha's Paphnutius, by Oswald R. Kuehne, A," 103
Sturm, P. Ambros, 100
"Südenfall und Umkehr der Klausnerin Maria" (The Fall and Conversion of the Recluse Maria), 37. *See also Abraham*
"Suora Hrosvita," 94
Supplementum de scriptoribus vel de scriptis ecclesiasticis a Bellarmino omissis: Ad annum 1460, 81
Susato, 41
Syntagma de constructione coenobii Gandesiani, 59, 60, 61, 62, 97, 108
Szilágyi, Sándor, 48, 93

Tablet, The, 74
Tablet, The, a Catholic weekly, 108
Tägtmeyer, Karl, 36, 39
"Tausendjahrfeier zu Gandersheim," 104
Taylor, J. R., 75
Taylor, Lily Ross, 40
Teatro e la Latinità di Hrotsvitha, Il, 108

"Teatro e la Latinità di Hrot-svitha per M. Rigobon, Il," 106, 109, 116
Teatro scelto, 74
Tecchi, Bonaventura, 106
Temps, Le, 35, 95
Tenth-century dramatist: Ros-witha the nun, A," 99, 101
Terence, 12, 19, 21
" 'Terentian' comedies of a tenth-century nun, The," 106
"Terentius Christianus: Hrot-svitha," 110
Terry, Ellen, 35–36
Texan Review, 102
Textkritisches zu Hrotsvit, 99
"Thaïs," 37, 38. *See also Paph-nutius*
Thaïs, 26
Thankmar of Hildesheim, 4, 55
Theatre Annual, The, 117
Theatre Arts Monthly, 106
"Théâtre de Hrosvita traduit par M. Charles Magnin," 85
Théâtre de Hrotsvitha, 68
"Théâtre de Hrotswitha," 89
Théâtre Européen: Théâtre an-térieur à la Renaissance, 68
Themar, Adam Wernher von, 47, 84, 93, 98, 108
Theologisches Literaturblatt, 89
Theophano, 9
Theophilus, 42
  printed editions, 74, 75
"Three Christian Maidens," 107
" 'Tibicines' nella poesia di Hrotsvitha, I," 112
Tillyard, H. J. W., 36, 73
Toldy, Ferencz, 48, 52, 87
Tolk, Edmund E., 108
Tonneelarbeid eener non uit de teinde eeuw, De (The Dramatic Works of a Nun of the Tenth Century), 94
Toneelgids, 106
Traube, 43
Traut, Wolf, 57
Tritheim, Johannes, 78, 80, 82, 100
Trümper, Bernarda, 99
Tutto il teatro, 77

"Über das Verhältnis von Hrotsuits Gesta Oddonis zu Widukind," 90
"Über den Ligurinus,"91

"Über Klüpfels Werk," 84
Über Roswitha's Carmen de Gestis Oddonis, 92
Unbekannte Hrotsvitha-Handschrift, Eine," 104
Ungherini, Aglauro, 96
Unterkircher, Dr. Franz, 56

Valentini, Guiseppe, 116
Varia carmina, 78
Varius, 48
Vellini, C., 72
Verzeichnisse der lateinischen Handschriften, 99
Veterum Scriptorum, qui Caesarum et imperatorum Germanicorum res per aliquot secula gestas literis mandarunt, Tomus unus . . ., 58
Veterum scriptorum . . . tomus unus, a Iusto Reubero olim editus, nova hac editione . . . curante Georgio Christiano Ioannis, 64
Vie littéraire, La, 95
Vignola, Bruno, 105
Villemain, Abel François, 84
Virgil, 12, 13
Vision [Revelation] of St. John, 3, 113
  manuscripts, 42, 43
  printed editions, 57, 69, 70, 71, 75
Vita, by Agius, 7
Vita (Anon.), 17–18
Vita Bernwardi, 55
"Vita Mathildis Reginae II," 105
Vitae paparum SS. Anastasii et Innocentii, 42, 54
Volf, György, 49
Vom Altertum zur Gegenwart, die Kulturzusammenhange in den Hauptepochen und auf der Hauptgebieten: Literatur, 102
"Von der Tausendjährigen Hrotswitha-Stadt Ganders-heim," 105
Vorspiel: Gesammelte Schriften zur Geschichte des deutschen Geistes, 103
Vossius, Gerhard Johannes, 81

Waddell, Helen, 105
Waitz, Georg, 56, 89, 90, 91
Walderdorff, Hugo Franz Philipp Wilder von, 92

Waley, Arthur, 36
Walsh, Gerald Groveland, S. J., 109
Walther, H., 75
Wandering Scholars, The, 105
Wattenbach, Ernst Christian Wilhelm, 70, 87, 91
Waysblum, Dr. Marek, 61, 90
Wedeck, Harry Ezekiel, 106
Weiss, Konrad, 115
Weitzmann-Fiedler, Dr. J., 56
Wendelgard, Abbess of Gan-dersheim, 8
"Were Hrostvitha's dramas performed during his [sic] lifetime?" 114
Werke (Barack), 70
Werke (Homeyer), 75
"Werke der Hrotsvitha herausgegeben von K. A. Barack, Die," 86
"Wernher von Themar, ein Heidelberger Humanist," 93
Widukind Korvei, 58
Widukind von Korvei, ein Bei-trag zur Kritik der Geschichts-schreiber des X Jahrhunderts, 88
Wiedererweckung der Drusiana und des Calimachus, Die, 75
Wiegand, Sister M. Gonsalva, O.S.F., 13, 41, 76
Wilken, Friedrich, 83
Wille, Jakob, 98
William, Archbishop of Mainz, 22, 55
Williams, Jane, 87
Winkler, Friedrich, 57
Winterfeld, Paul Karl Rudolf von, 35, 42, 43, 71, 72, 97, 99
Wissenschaftliche Vorträge ge-halten zu München, in Mün-chen, im Winter 1858, 87
Wolfenbüttel Ms 19. 13. Aug. 4°, 59
Women Under Monasticism, 96
"Works of Hroswitha, The," 56, 57, 113
Wüstemann, Justin Elias, 82

Young, Karl, 109

Zapiski po istorii zapadno-evropeiskikh literatur . . . (Notes on the History of Western European Litera-tures . . .), 101

Zeichnungen Albrecht Dürers, Die, 57
Zeitschrift des Harz-Vereins für Geschichte und Alterthumskunde, 93
Zeitschrift für Bibliothekswissen und Bibliographie (in Russian: *Zhurnal bibliotekoznavstva ta bibliografii*), 112
Zeitschrift für deutsche Bildung, 108
Zeitschrift für deutsches Altertum und deutsche Literatur, 97, 103, 104
Zeitschrift für die Geschichte des Oberrheins, 93
Zell, C., 84
Zeydel, Edwin Herman, 58, 63, 64, 75, 78, 112, 113, 114
Zhurnal ministerstva narodnogo prosviasccheniia, SPB (Journal of the Ministry of Education, SPB), 91
Zint, Bruno, 92
Zolnai, Gyula, 49, 96
"Zu Hrosvithas Wirkungskreis," 105
"Zu Hrotsvits Theophilus v. 17," 97
"Zur Hrotsvit von Gandersheim," 77
"Zur Hrotswithfrage," 90
"Zur Tausendjahrfeier von Gandersheim: Sachsen und die Dichtung Hrotsvits," 104
Zuverlässige Nachrichten von den vornehmsten Schriftstellern vom Anfange der Welt bis 1500, 83

Twelve hundred copies of this book have been printed
for the Hroswitha Club in December 1965.
It has been composed in English Monotype Bell,
and printed and bound by Clarke & Way, Inc.
at the Thistle Press in New York.